PERCUSSION:

A Course of Study for the Future
Band and Orchestra Director

Second Edition
by T. Siwe

Student Workbook

Media Press, Inc.

A special thank you to the following for their help in preparing these pages for publication: Ron Coulter, Dr. Dan DeSena, Dr. Kathleen Kastner, Terrance Mayhue and Dr. Glenn Schaft.

Also, thanks to the following companies and individuals for providing illustration sources: Black Swamp Percussion and Eric Sooy, photographer; Christopher Cree; Frederick Fairchild; Vic Firth Mallets; Grover Pro Percussion; B. Kolberg Percussion Instruments; Johnny Lane; Latin Percussion; Ludwig-Musser; David Madden; William Moersch; Remo, Inc.; Sonar Drums; Marian Wyatt; Yamaha USA; A. Zildjian Co.

to my wife, Joan Rebecca

Media Press, Inc.
1341 W. Fullerton Ave., #355
Chicago, IL 60614
U.S.A.

For more information contact: www.mediapressinc.com

Printed in the United States of America

ISBN: 978 0-9635891-6-3

Contents

IV. Bass Drum

V. Cymbals

VI. Timpani

VII. Triangle

VIII. Tambourine

Introduction

A Course of Study for the Future Band and Orchestra Director

The purpose of this course of study is to provide music educators with basic information concerning teaching methods and performance techniques for musical instruments common to the percussion family. Future band and orchestra directors will follow a course of study that, upon completion, will enable them to teach beginning students at the public school elementary or secondary levels, and to continue to provide said students with an accepted, organized approach to learning and developing percussion techniques and skills.

This course is designed to acquaint the music educator with the most commonly used percussion instruments. Included are the snare drum, the timpani and those instruments that comprise the mallet-keyboard group, i.e. xylophone, marimba, vibraphone, orchestra bells and tubular chimes. Percussion instruments such as the triangle, tambourine, castanets and others common to the literature are also presented. Special sections deal with the drum set, marching percussion and ethnic instruments, all of which are important to today's school music program. Brief histories are given for each instrument along with a discussion of their acoustical properties and notational idiosyncrasies. Finally, a syllabus with recommended readings from various standard percussion texts, lists of resources and reference materials and some useful elementary and high school percussion ensembles provide additional information.

To understand and to teach beginning percussion techniques, it is important that the music educator go through the process of learning basic performance skills. Without at least attempting to attain a modicum of performance ability on each of the major percussion instruments, a future teacher will lack the knowledge and insight that comes only through this process. For each instrument or area, graduated exercises and etudes provide step-by-step learning. Through this accelerated course of study, student music educators will develop performance skills on snare drum, drum set, timpani, the mallet-keyboard instruments and many of the other percussion instruments common to the repertoire. As they do so, they will formulate an approach to teaching the beginning percussionist while increasing their own efficacy in the studio, in the classroom and on the podium.

Course Requirements

Students are required to attend class regularly due to the course's practical, laboratory approach. A modest amount of outside reading is required from library reference books and other information sources, but to gain the required level of performance ability, knowledge and insight that comes with this process, considerable time must be devoted to individual practice. Students must purchase their own snare drum sticks and bring them to each class meeting. Students will be informed of the need for any additional class material. The location and use of practice facilities will be discussed during the first class meeting.

Syllabus

Course Description

The purpose of this course is to provide music educators with basic information concerning teaching methods and performance techniques for musical instruments common to the percussion family. Students will follow a course of study that will enable them to teach beginning students at the elementary or secondary school levels and to continue to provide them with an accepted, organized approach to learning and developing percussion techniques and skills.

This course of study is designed to acquaint students with the history of each major instrument found in the percussion family, their acoustical properties and methods of sound production, and the idiosyncrasies of percussion music notation. It will provide future band and orchestra directors with a rudimentary technique on many of the instruments labeled percussion, concentrating on those that are most common to today's elementary and high school band and orchestra literature.

Course Requirements

Students will be required to attend class regularly due to the course's practical, laboratory approach. A minimal amount of outside reading will be required from reference books found in your library. Considerable time must be devoted to individual practice. With the exception of snare drum sticks, all mallets and beaters needed for class and for practice as well as a practice pad and locker will be provided. Equipment and mallets will be assigned to each student who then assumes responsibility for any loss or damage. Replacement or repair costs will be assessed as losses and damages occur.

Reading List

Written tests will include questions based upon the information given in this book plus information from class lectures. Readings from other reference materials indicated will help give you additional insights and depth of understanding. It is recommended that you explore as much of this reading material as possible.

Terminology: idiophones, membranophones, pitched and non-pitched percussion.
Read: related sections of Siwe's *Percussion: A Course of Study...*

Basic sound production: striking, scraping, rubbing, bowing, shaking.
Read: related sections of Siwe's *Percussion: A Course of Study...*

Notation: problems with the acoustic properties of percussion instruments.
Read: related sections of Siwe's *Percussion: A Course of Study...*

Percussion Auditions: testing coordination and aural skills; talent evaluations
Read: related sections of Siwe's *Percussion: A Course of Study...*; Gary D. Cook. *Teaching Percussion*: pp.11-12.

A Model Course of Study: individual/class lessons, course outline.
Read: related sections of Siwe's *Percussion: A Course of Study...*

Organizing the Percussion Section: leadership, equipment, part assignments.
Read: related sections of Siwe's *Percussion: A Course of Study...*

Snare Drum: history, construction/nomenclature, tuning, sizes, stands, stance, sticks, grips; performance techniques: playing areas/tone production, basic motions, notation, idiomatic patterns, sticking policy, embellishments, flams, drags, ruffs, rim-shots
Read: related sections of Siwe's *Percussion: A Course of Study...*; Gary D. Cook. *Teaching Percussion:* topic related parts from pp. 24-68

Bass Drum: history, construction and nomenclature, sizes, stands, tuning, sticks and mallets, grips, stance/dampening; performance techniques: playing area, tone production, stroke motions, notation, sticking.
Read: related sections of Siwe's *Percussion: A Course of Study...*; Gary D. Cook. *Teaching Percussion:* pp. 215-224

Cymbals: history, nomenclature, selecting cymbals, weight and sizes, straps and pads, grip, stance; performance techniques: solo crash, keeping time, articulation, suspended cymbal.
Read: related sections of Siwe's *Percussion: A Course of Study...*, Albert Payson & Jack McKenzie. *Music Educators' Guide to Teaching Percussion,* Sec. V

Timpani: history, models, construction, nomenclature, standard set of drums, mallets, sticks, grips; performance techniques: playing areas, stroke actions, tuning, dampening, mutes, notation, forte-piano rolls, sticking.
Read: related sections of Siwe's *Percussion: A Course of Study...*

Triangle: history, types, sizes, beaters, suspension; performance techniques: strokes, embellishments.
Read: related sections of Siwe's *Percussion: A Course of Study...*

Tambourine: history, sizes, models, grip; performance techniques: slow-loud, slow-soft, fast-loud, fast-soft, rolls (shake and thumb), embellishments, playing with snare sticks.
Read: related sections of Siwe's *Percussion: A Course of Study...*

Castanets: history, types (hand held, machine, paddle), grips; performance techniques: traditional Spanish, articulation, rolls (knee, wrist).
Read: related sections of Siwe's *Percussion: A Course of Study...;* Gary D. Cook. *Teaching Percussion:* pp. 240-241

Claves: history, types, sizes; performance techniques: hand grip, open & closed sound.
Read: related sections of Siwe's *Percussion: A Course of Study...;* Gary D. Cook. *Teaching Percussion:* pp. 265-66

Ratchet: history, types and sizes; performance techniques: dynamics.
Read: related sections of Siwe's *Percussion: A Course of Study...*; Gary D. Cook. *Teaching Percussion:* p. 246

Slapstick (whip): history, types and sizes; performance techniques: spring, non-spring.
Read: related sections of Siwe's *Percussion: A Course of Study...;* Gary D. Cook. *Teaching Percussion:* p. 245

Slit Drums (log drums): history, types, mallets; performance techniques: stroke, striking area.
Read: related sections of Siwe's *Percussion: A Course of Study...;* Gary D. Cook. *Teaching Percussion:* p. 248

Temple Blocks: history, sets and sizes, stands, mallets and sticks; performance techniques: playing area, special effects.
Read: related sections of Siwe's *Percussion: A Course of Study...;* Read: James Blades. *Percussion Instruments and their History.* pp. 390-397

Woodblocks: history, types and sizes, mallets; performance techniques: striking area.
Read: related sections of Siwe's *Percussion: A Course of Study...;* Gary D. Cook. *Teaching Percussion:* p. 242

Anvil: history, types, substitutions, beaters; performance techniques: striking areas, tone production, safety concerns.
Read: related sections of Siwe's *Percussion: A Course of Study...;*

Cowbells: history, types (Latin, agogo (double, triple) Kentucky, almglocken), mallets, beaters, sticks, stands and other suspension devices; performance techniques: striking areas, tone production, articulation, time keeping.
Read: related sections of Siwe's *Percussion: A Course of Study...;* Gary D. Cook. *Teaching Percussion:* p. 273

Crotales: history, range, mallets, repertoire; performance techniques: striking areas, tone production, vibrato
Read: related sections of Siwe's *Percussion: A Course of Study...;* Gary D. Cook. *Teaching Percussion:* p. 104

Gongs: history, types, sizes, suspension, beaters; performance techniques: playing area, tone production, strokes, dampening, rolls, articulation.
Read: related sections of Siwe's *Percussion: A Course of Study...;* Gary D. Cook. *Teaching Percussion:* pp. 239-240

Tam tams: history, types, sizes, suspension, beaters; performance techniques: playing area, tone production, dampening, rolls, articulation.
Read: related sections of Siwe's *Percussion: A Course of Study...*

Marimba: history, range, sound, mallets, grips; performance techniques: striking areas, tone production, stance, sticking, notation.
Read: related sections of Siwe's *Percussion: A Course of Study...;* Gary D. Cook. *Teaching Percussion:* pp. 128-129

Xylophone: history, range, sound, mallets, grips; performance techniques: playing area, tone production, sticking, notation.
Read: related sections of Siwe's *Percussion: A Course of Study...*

Vibraphone: history, range, mallets, grips; performance techniques; pedaling, playing areas, tone production, sticking, notation.
Read: related sections of Siwe's *Percussion: A Course of Study...*

Orchestra Bells: (Glockenspiel): history, range, mallets, grips; performance techniques, playing areas, tone production, sticking, notation.
Read: related sections of Siwe's *Percussion: A Course of Study...*

Tubular Bells (Tubular Chimes): performance techniques: stroke, strike area, dampening.
Read: related sections of Siwe's *Percussion: A Course of Study...*

Drum Set: history, components of the drum set, hardware, sticks; performance techniques: coordination exercises, styles: Funk, Latin, Swing, Shuffle, Rock.
Read: related sections of Siwe's *Percussion: A Course of Study...*; Encyclopedia of Percussion. John H. Beck, editor. pp. 174-183

Rattles and Shakers: history, types (afuché, cabaça, caxixi, chocalho, maracas, quijada, shekeré, vibraslap); performance techniques: dynamics, articulation.
Read: related sections of Siwe's *Percussion: A Course of Study...*; Gary D. Cook. *Teaching Percussion:* pp. 274-277

Scrapers and Raspers: history, types (guiro, guira, reco-reco); performance techniques, scrape, tap.
Read: related sections of Siwe's *Percussion: A Course of Study...*

Bongos and Congas: history, types, sizes; performance techniques: hands, sticks.
Read: related sections of Siwe's *Percussion: A Course of Study...*

Marching Percussion: history, philosophy, equipment, instrumentation; performance techniques: uniformity, marching and drill formations, cadences.
Read: related sections of Siwe's *Percussion: A Course of Study...*; Gary D. Cook. *Teaching Percussion:* pp. 420-424

Reading Assignment References

Beck, John H. , ed., 1995 *Encyclopedia of Percussion*. New York: Garland Publishing, Inc.

Blades, James. 1970. *Percussion Instruments and their History*. New York: Frederick A. Praeger, Publishers.

Cook, Gary D. 2006 *Teaching Percussion,* Third Edition. Belmont, California. Thomson Schirmer.

Payson, Albert and Jack McKenzie. 1976. *Percussion in the School Music Program*. Park Ridge, Illinois: Payson Percussion Products.

Siwe, Thomas. 2007. *Percussion: A Course of Study for the Future Band and Orchestra Director*. Second Edition. Chicago: Media Press, Inc.

The History of Percussion Instruments and Their Solo and Ensemble Literature

"The story of the rise and development of percussion instruments is closely linked with the history of mankind and may justly claimed to have exercised a tremendous influence on the human race." (Blades 1970, 33).

Drums have been ubiquitous throughout the history of humankind. Seen on Sumerian reliefs as early as 2500 B.C., drums performed various functions in numerous ancient cultures throughout the world. Revered as gods, they often served as symbols of war, their sounds bringing fear to the enemy. They were used as instruments of communication both in the jungles of Africa and by the armies of the American Revolution. The sound of drumming accompanied songs and dances, provided music for rituals of death as well as for celebration. From the earliest of times, percussion instruments have been found in societies throughout the world comprising the majority of the instruments used by man.

Yet it wasn't until the early Christian era that the basic percussion instruments used in today's music began to appear in the West, brought into Europe by traders, soldiers and migrating peoples. In the Eleventh Century, the Crusaders brought home the captured kettledrums of the Saracens. Originating in India, these ornate instruments, symbols of military leadership and power, were much smaller and more shallow than today's orchestra timpani. Over the next 900 years, the timpani were developed and refined into today's copper clad set of four drums seen at the rear of most orchestras and concert bands.

Playing the kettle drums takes a great deal of technical skill and musicianship. Over nine hundred years ago, kettle drummers and their trumpeter colleagues were the elite of secular musicians. Guilds supporting the royal trumpeters and kettle drummers provided schooling which took as long as four years before an aspirant drummer could take the examination for guild certification. As early as 1685, a work for two kettle drummers was composed by the French percussionist, Andre Philidor. Fanfares, entrances and interludes were written for trumpets and timpani providing music for the king and his court. Solo displays by timpani virtuosi were part of the royal music of the European courts during the Baroque period.

In 1720 the Sultan of Turkey sent a full Janissary band to the Polish court. The percussion instruments included bass drum, tambourine and triangle. Within fifty years, "Turkish Music" was the rage throughout Europe; every military band had its Turkish music. Mozart's overture to *The Abduction from the Seraglio* reflected this interest in the exotic East. Beethoven used triangle, bass drum and cymbals, in addition to pauken (German for timpani) in the last movement of his *Ninth Symphony*.

Significant advances in the percussive arts in the early nineteenth century were realized not so much by increasing the number of instruments used by the Western orchestra as by refining the playing techniques. Haydn had mastered the kettledrums and took advantage of this knowledge in his later symphonies. Both he and Mozart insisted on exactness of tuning. Beethoven pushed the technical requirements of the kettledrums even further calling for more notes than just the root of tonic and dominant chords. In response to the need for more frequent tuning changes, a German craftsman, Gerhard Cramer, in 1812, developed a device that enabled the drums to be tuned with the twist of just one screw. Within a century, the machine-cranked timpani evolved into pedal-controlled, tunable drums.

During the 19th century, the Romantics and the nationalist composers brought to the orchestra more and more percussion instruments, a trend which in fact continues to this day. Percussion instruments were often scored in Western orchestras in the following ways. Various drums were used to accompany dance-like melodies just as they did in folk music. Tambourines and finger cymbals evoked the memory of gypsy caravans camped outside of town. The snare drum, bass drum and cymbals reminded listeners of marching troops. The tolling chimes represented the church, death, or the passing of time. Spanish castanets brought forth the image of Flamenco dancers. Gongs and xylophones created the atmosphere of the mysterious Orient, and so forth. Composers used percussion instruments in these ways to bring extra-musical ideas to the listener.

One of the most famous orchestration books of the late nineteenth century suggested to the composer that the bass drum was to be used very sparingly when writing a symphony: once in the first movement; never in the middle movements, and no more than three times in the finale. When one wanted to put a period on the end of a musical sentence, a sforzando written for bass drum and cymbals acted as an exclamation mark. A low tam tam note was most thought provoking and the triangle 'ding' at the end of a harp glissando left us holding our breath.

Thus percussion was used by composers not just to keep time or to mark the beat as first comes to mind, but also to set the scene and to help end the musical phrase. These three traditional uses of percussion by Western composers began to change early in the 20th century when a new generation of composers, looking for new and original ways to express themselves, began to reevaluate the parameters of music. German critic Stuckenschmidt pointed out that: "The generation of composers around the year 1900 was no longer caught up in the battle between 'pure music' and 'music drama'. The war it had to wage was situated on a quite different level, and its critical implications have proved more considerable: what was really at stake for this generation was the very validity of music's raw material." (Buchet-Chastel 1956, 9).

In Europe, Igor Stravinsky caused the Paris audiences to riot with his *Le Sacre du Printemps* (1913). More important to the percussionist was Stravinsky's orchestration of the "Soldiers Tale" (*Histoire du soldat*) five years later. Here the percussionist was asked to play more than one instrument at a time. In fact, he or she was asked to play a bass drum, two snare drums, tenor drum, tambourine, triangle and cymbal in a musical setting that, with its poly-meters and dissonant harmonies, challenged musician as well as listener. In Italy, less than a week after the premiere of *Le Sacre*, the artist/composer Luigi Russolo gave a concert of Futurist music using his newly created *Intonarumori* -noise intoners - machines that could create scales of gurgles, screams, roars, twitters, etc. Both Stravinsky and Russolo offered listeners something new: percussive sounds for their own intrinsic value.

Other important European composers that helped change the way percussion was orchestrated included the Hungarian Bela Bartok with his *Sonata for Two Pianos and Percussion* (1937) and Darius Milhaud, one of the French Six, with a work for chamber orchestra, *La Creation du Monde,* that included the saxophone, plus an early version of the drum set he had seen and heard used in Harlem during a visit to New York. In the United States, a young pianist/composer, Henry Cowell, was playing the piano with fists and elbows while another Paris riot was set off by the American George Anthiel with his *Ballet mecanique*, scored for airplane propeller sounds, electric bells, eight player pianos, four xylophones and percussion. On March 9, 1933 in New York City, the composer/musicologist Nicholas Slonimsky conducted the world premiere of a work composed two years earlier in Paris, the now classic Varèse *Ionisation*. On that same Pan American Association concert a fugue for percussion by the American composer, William Russell, was played.

By the 1950s, a substantial body of work existed for the percussion ensemble and visionary pedagogues quickly brought this genre into college music programs, precipitating a deluge of new compositions for public school music programs. Solo literature was soon to follow.

The xylophone was the first mallet-keyboard instrument to attract western composers. African or Asian in origin, its western version was at first a simple array of wooden bars laid upon a bed of straw (straw fiddle). In the early 1800s, the Russian xylophonist Gusikov created a sensation with his performances in the salons of Europe, as noted by the composers Chopin and Liszt. The xylophone also captured the imagination of the French composer, Saint Saens, whose *Danse Macabre* (1874) is an early use of the xylophone in an orchestra setting, preceded by the less known Moravian composer, Ferdinand Kauer, who wrote the cantata *Der Einsiedler* (1805), which included a substantive xylophone part. In the United States, the xylophone found a place in vaudeville and became a popular solo instrument during the early days of recordings, 1890-1930. Solo artists, such as George Hamilton Green championed the use of the xylophone, concertizing throughout the land and recording transcriptions as well as original works. The J. C. Deagan company of Chicago, Illinois provided new and improved instruments, later adding a line of marimbas, orchestra bells and inventing the now popular vibraphone.

Soon after its invention, the vibraphone found a home with the jazz bands of the early twentieth century. Jazz "vibes" artists such as Red Norvo, Lionel Hampton and Terry Gibbs developed techniques and found ways to express the new jazz sounds via a three octave set of tuned aluminum bars with a mechanical set of rotating baffles set in the top of resonating tubes. Today's vibraphone (aka vibraharp) continues to evolve with new innovative models and champions such as recording artist Gary Burton.

The marimba, which is a wooden bar instrument similar to the xylophone, was "an essential element of the musical life of Guatemala and has been since the mid-nineteenth century" (Kastner 1989, 9). Latin artists such as Jose Bethancourt and the Hurtado family helped popularize the marimba through performances at concerts, festivals and on radio programs. Composers such as Paul Creston, Darius Milhaud and Robert Kurka wrote early concerti for marimba with orchestra. Soloists and teachers, such as Vida Chenoweth and Clair Omar Musser, brought the instrument new respectability. Since the late twentieth century, the marimba has become the standard mallet training instrument for percussionists, with an enormous body of solo and ensemble literature for both the professional and educational market.

Today's percussionist is regarded by many as a figure symbolizing the changes in the musical arts that have taken place in recent times. Though many of the percussion instruments are ancient in origin, contemporary players and composers continue to explore their musical potential.

Terminology

Definitions of terms unique to percussion instruments.

It is helpful to classify percussion instruments as follows: idiophones, membranophones, tuned and non-tuned instruments.

membranophone: "An instrument in which sound is produced by the vibration of a membrane, traditionally a stretched animal skin, though now often a synthetic material." (Randel 1986, 485) Instruments common to this classification would be the snare drum, bass drum, timpani, tom-toms, congas, etc..

Idiophone: "Any musical instrument that produces sound by the vibration of its own primary material" (Randel 1986, 389)). Percussion instruments common to this classification include: cymbals, castanets and claves (concussion idiophones); bells, xylophones, wood blocks (percussion idiophones); maracas, sleighbells (rattles); guiros, ratchets (scrapers); marimbulas, mbiras (plucked idiophones); musical saw (friction idiophone)

Note: It is possible for an instrument to fall into both categories, i.e. membranophone and idiophone. For example, the tambourine's sound is created by striking its head which causes metal disks (jingles) attached to its frame to rattle. Any membrane instrument can be used as an idiophone by striking its rim, frame, or shell.

Pitched percussion: Percussion instruments that fall into the category of pitched percussion include idiophones such as orchestra bells (glockenspiel), xylophone, marimba, vibraphone, tubular chimes, crotales, steel drum, handbells, gongs and membranophones such as timpani and roto-toms. Composers use these instruments for both their unique timbre as well as their ability to provide a recognizable pitch.

Non-pitched percussion: The majority of percussion instruments fall into the category of non-pitched, or indefinite pitch and include idiophones such as wood block, log drum, slapstick, ratchet, cymbal, tam tam, castanet, triangle, temple blocks and membraphones such as snare drum, tenor drum, field drum, bass drum, tom-tom and conga. Composers and arrangers often write for groups of non-pitched percussion, such as an array of three or four tom-toms or a set of Korean temple blocks. Care must be taken to 'tune' or adjust the pitch areas or intervals between the instruments so that any audible scale implied by the intervalic relationship of these so called 'non-pitched' instruments fits into the tonal fabric of the composition being played.

Many of the percussion instruments designated as 'non-pitched' in fact possess specific pitches. Tom-toms (especially single-headed toms), wood blocks (especially temple blocks and slit drums), metallic instruments such as triangles, cowbells, and even small tam tams can be and are perceived by the listener as being pitched. Some composers are aware of this phenomenon and take care to avoid unwanted implied scales and other audible pitch relationships by specifying exact pitches for many of the so-called non-pitched percussion instruments, but most do not. They leave it up to the player and/or conductor to avoid this problem by selecting or retuning instruments so as not to create undesirable scales or pitches.

Basic Sound Production

(striking, scraping , rubbing, bowing, shaking, etc.)

Percussionists activate the various instruments found in the percussion section using a variety of disparate   physical actions. For example, to play the snare drum, the hands and arms move in a relaxed, coordinated way, much as a swimmer doing the crawl. To crash the cymbals or shake a tambourine much different movements are required, ones that take both tension and relaxation.

It is important for the percussion student to learn which physical action is used to produce a desired sound as well as which sticks or mallets or other activators are necessary and appropriate for the occasion. Generally, one must use a stick or mallet that has the correct mass and weight appropriate for each of the percussion instruments. One would not normally strike a snare drum with a large bass drum or tam tam beater, nor would one use metal bell mallets on a conga drum or marimba; such actions would result in poor sound quality and may, in fact, damage the instrument or break a head.

In addition, you will find that <u>where</u> one strikes, rubs or scrapes a percussion instrument is critical to the resultant sound. On some percussion instruments, such as the triangle or marimba, a centimeter off the striking target will audibly change the sound produced. Professional percussionists spend hours of practice time perfecting their stroke, much as a golf pro, so that they are able to strike the instrument in just the right place.

Thus, <u>how</u> to strike, scrape, rub, or pluck; <u>what </u>to use in the way of sticks or mallets; and <u>where</u> to touch or hit a percussion instrument are basic questions the percussionist must answer. As an instructor or conductor, this knowledge is of vital importance.

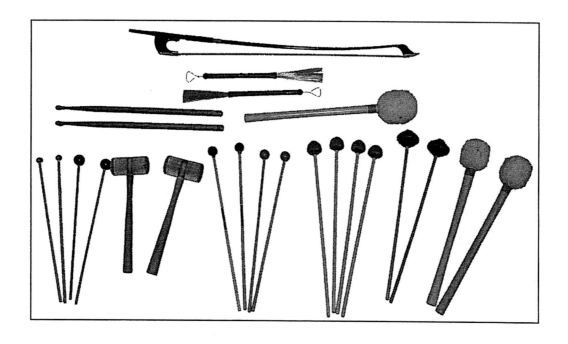

Percussion Notation

Composers have, over centuries, found unique ways to convey their musical creations and to capture the essence of their ideas on paper. Putting these musical creations on paper became more precise after the introduction of mensural notation in the 16th century. The need to do so was obvious. For voices and groups of instruments to perform together it was efficient for the composer to notate the music on paper, rather than teach every part by rote.

As percussion instruments began to be notated, composers and music editors adapted to their use the notations developed earlier for voices, strings and other instruments. However, the short staccato notes of the snare drum, or even the more lengthy sound decay of the bass drum and cymbals, made it very difficult or impractical to exactly notate their duration. Still today, it is impossible to find one notation that works for all percussion instruments. Kurt Stone says: "It is neither practical nor, in fact, possible to notate exact durations of short-decay instruments." (Stone 1980, 220)

Since all of you either sing or play another instrument, select a piece of music that is familiar to you and imagine its rhythms played on the snare drum. A notated whole note, half note, quarter note, eighth note when played all sound the same. The same series of notes played on the triangle could be controlled using a dampening technique, but each note would have a built-in diminuendo. Percussion students must learn how to deal with inexact notation. Knowledge of idiomatic writing and the traditions of interpretation are critical to the percussionist's training.

Percussion instruments that have lengthy sound decay need to be controlled or they will interfere with the music. Developing techniques to dampen their decay is as important as learning to create a good sound. The percussionist learns that the cymbal or triangle sound is sometimes allowed to follow its natural decay, but more often needs to be controlled in such a manner as to match the durations of the other musical instruments heard with it, regardless of the notation.

Often the music notated in the percussionist's part is so fragmentary as to suggest improvisation. Drum set notation is often no more than a written description of the style with occasional accents or cues. Here the player brings the notation to the music. Knowledge of notated percussion music is as important to the drum set student as to other percussionists. All pedagogic drum set material, even that with play-along electronic accompaniment, include fully notated musical examples that the player memorizes and uses to fill out the often sketchy drum set charts.

In recent times, composers have used a staff notation that combines a multitude of pitched and non-pitched percussion arranged in an order unique to that composition. Thus the percussion player cannot rely on a standard notation, one that is basically the same for each piece of music. Today's percussionist must cope with inexact notation better suited for voice, wind or string instruments. He or she must be trained to be aware of a multitude of performance traditions and musical styles and a great variety of notational systems.

Percussion Auditions

Selecting a beginning percussion student

Each school instrumental music director faces the challenge of screening and selecting students who are interested in band or orchestra but who do not play an instrument. The music director's busy schedule rarely leaves time for extensive interviews and examination. Yet they know that it is important to both the potential student and to the school's music program to make a serious effort to match the desires of the student with the needs of the program. The following important testing areas can be covered in a short period of time and will benefit both the student and the program.

Intelligence

A quick survey of the student's prior school records will help select the future percussionist. It is important that during the interview the student demonstrates poise and maturity at a level that would enable him/her to play instruments that are usually solo, i.e. cymbals, timpani, bells, bass drum, etc.).

Motor skills

Obviously you want a future percussionist to have basic coordination. A simple test of clapping hands while marching in time should demonstrate this capability. Keeping time, doubling time and producing easy rhythmic patterns by using both right and left hands will also demonstrate the necessary motor skills.

Aural skills

It is very important that today's percussionist have a good sense of pitch discrimination. A brief ear test (e.g., matching pitches, singing a simple melodic line, etc.) is a necessary part in selecting the future school percussionist, as important as demonstrating any motor or rhythmic skills.

Talent

To test for aptitude, the future percussionist should be able to repeat simple rhythmic phrases that you present. Try using music examples from beginning band and orchestra music. This will also give an indication as to the students learning potential and intelligence.

Auditions are part of music at every level. To ignore the importance of the audition process at the beginning level is an invitation to failure for the student and can be a potential problem for you, the director. Given the competitive nature of young groups of musicians, placing a student in a learning program without first testing to see if he or she has some possibility of success may place the student at risk, or at the very least, will be a waste of precious time.

A Model Course of Study for Beginning Percussionists

Two important rules must be observed when working with beginning students.

1. No student should be allowed, or expected, to play in the band or orchestra unless they have had instruction on that specific instrument. As you proceed through this course of study, you will find that each percussion instrument has specific techniques: how to hold, how to strike, how to dampen the sound, etc. It is wrong to assume, as many do, that lessons on the snare drum will produce a good bass drum or cymbal player.

2. Practice time at school on the large instruments, such as timpani, chimes, vibraphones, etc., must be made available for percussion students. Students cannot be expected to perform adequately on instruments on which they have not spent time practicing, ones that they touch only in rehearsals and in concerts.

Individual Lessons vs. Class Lessons

Individual lessons, of course, are the best way to teach music, however, time constraints may make class lessons the only alternative. Bringing your percussion students together for class lessons in which they play as a group can greatly assist you with your instructional goals. Today there is a great deal of excellent chamber percussion music available at all levels, from beginning to professional, for every conceivable combination of percussion instruments. You will find that a small ensemble affords you the opportunity to stop and correct, or to give instant instructions on how to play a given instrument, benefiting both the individual and the group. The percussion ensemble is a good medium in which to teach musicianship. It supplements training and functions as a laboratory where parts from large ensembles such as band or orchestra can be rehearsed. A separate rehearsal for your percussionists will help to build esprit de corps, reducing discipline problems. It can also serve as a time for maintenance, doing small repairs (such as restringing triangle clips or changing snare drum heads) while teaching students to respect and care for the equipment. Make it part of the following program.

Plan of Study

Level One: (Each level equates to 1 school year.)
Lessons: Snare drum, bass drum, small instruments, general music concepts and terms, theory/ear training.
Plays: Bass drum, small instruments, secondary snare drum parts.

Level Two:
Lessons: Mallet-keyboard instruments, cymbals, snare drum, theory/ear training.
Plays: Cymbals, snare drum, elementary bell parts.

Level Three:
Lessons: Timpani, mallet-keyboard instruments, snare drum, theory/ear training
Plays: Snare drum, mallet-keyboard instruments, secondary timpani parts.

Level Four:
Lessons: Drum set, timpani, mallet-keyboard instruments, theory/ear training.
Plays: Timpani, mallet-keyboard instruments, drum set

The above plan assumes that the student has had no prior musical training. It is just one way of introducing the student to the percussion instruments that are normally used in school music programs. As you can see, the percussion student has more than one instrument to learn and many techniques to master. Placing the drum set and timpani at higher levels of study takes advantage of the student's developing musical ear and growing maturity. There are other approaches to the above, but all must take into account the diverse needs of the percussionist and the demands of the school's music program. Marching percussion will be addressed at a later time in this course of study

Organizing the Percussion Section

Section Leader:
Your percussion section personnel will always be comprised of students at different levels of skill and maturity. Selecting one to serve as section leader will save you time and, perhaps, be of help with minor discipline problems. Assign the student leader specific tasks such as storing percussion equipment after rehearsals, alerting you to the need for repairs, orientating new students, etc. The section leader will need your supervision, but can be of significant help to the harried music educator.

Equipment Storage:
Lockable, permanent storage for all the percussion instruments, large and small, located in the rehearsal area is the best solution. A movable storage container (a percussion cart) can help too. Commercial carts are available though all seem to lack adequate locks. Adding a hasp and combination lock is advised. The replacement and maintenance of percussion equipment needs the constant attention of the music educator. Maintenance is discussed in a separate chapter.

Part Assignments:
To help organize the student percussion section, as well as to aid the conductor, you will find a simple assignment chart to be invaluable. Across one side of your chart list the names of the student percussionists. Each student must be held responsible for finding and setting up the instruments needed to play their part. The section leader should not be given this task. Along the other side of your chart list the titles of the works being rehearsed. Using recommended abbreviations for each instrument and mallet needed, fill in the squares. A copy of this chart should be given to each percussionist. See following example.

TITLE →

PLAYER ➤

Snare Drum

Batter Head

Counter Hoop

Snare Head

Snare Release

Tension Rod

History: In the West, pictures and written descriptions of double-headed drums with snares appear as early as the 14th century (Blades & Montagu 1977, 5). During the first millennium, an early snare drum, the tabor, was used throughout Europe. It appeared in many sizes and shapes, sometimes with or without snares, one or two-headed, oft times played with one hand while the other held a pipe (small flute). The large version of the medieval tabor, " a double-headed, cord-tensioned drum with a single snare on the struck (batter) head" (Blades & Montagu 1977, 4) evolved into the snare drum later used by military bands. Slung from a shoulder strap, it hung waist high at about a 45° angle, with the barrel of the drum trailing along side the player (the side drum), its thick vellum (skin) heads struck with two stout wooden sticks. The angle of the batter head (top head) required the player to grip the left stick between the thumb and first finger with the palm up, while the right hand held the stick in a more natural manner. This traditional left hand grip continues to be used today especially in drum and fife bands. In recent times, modern drum carriers have made it possible for the marching player to use the matched grip (both hands use the right hand grip). The military snare drum not only played a role in the band, but was also used, along with bugles, to send signals to the troops and gun batteries. Calls such as *reveille, cease fire, dinner call, retreat*, were taught by rote and their rhythmic patterns are still part of the snare drum's idiomatic language. The size of the snare drum has been reduced over the years and its sensitivity increased. Wire, cable and various combinations replaced the old gut or cord snares, plastic heads are now used instead of animal skins and a mechanism has been added that allows the snare drummer to rapidly release the snares from contact with the bottom head (snare head).

Construction/Nomenclature: Snare drum shells are usually constructed from wood or metal, though synthetic versions are popular as well. Heads, made from sheets of plastic material, enclose the cylinder on both ends. An 'air hole' provides escape for the pressure changes that occur during playing. The plastic head material is molded onto a metal hoop called the "flesh hoop". The name derives from earlier days when heads were made from animal skin.

The top head, called the 'batter head', is thicker and thus more durable than the bottom, or snare head. Over each head is placed another hoop, the 'counter-hoop', which provides even tension to the heads. Through these counter-hoops are threaded 'tension rods' that screw into 'lugs' attached to the sides of the drum cylinder. Adjustment to the head tension is made by turning the tension rods evenly by means of a 'drum key'.

The snare drum takes its name from the strands of wire that run across the bottom head called 'snares.' Snares can be made from materials other than wire, such as nylon, gut, rope, or cable. The ends of the snares are passed through openings in the bottom counter-hoop and attached to opposite sides of the drum's shell. On one side a device called the 'snare strainer' holds the ends of the wires and provides a method to adjust the snare tension. Most snare drum strainers also have a release mechanism that enables the player to quickly turn the snares 'on' or 'off'.

Tuning: To get the best sound from your snare drum, it is important to 'tune' the drum and 'adjust' the snares so that your snare drum provides a sharp, resonant sound when struck. The amount of tension on the head at the point where each rod goes through the counter-hoop should be the same. You can check this by striking the drum head with a stick near each rod, adjusting the tension so that all sound the same. You can also use a mechanical device that measures the head tension. Both heads should be fairly tight, with the snare head a little looser than the batter head. The snares should be adjusted so that they lie snugly against the snare head. Too much tension will cause the snares to 'choke', too little tension will cause them to 'rattle' or 'buzz'.

Size: Drums with snares come in a variety of sizes. The following recommendations for concert snare drums are fairly standard.
5 1/2" x 14", or 6 1/2" x 14", for general concert use.
3 1/2 "x 14" piccolo drum. Useful when part calls for high and low snare drums.
12" x 15" field drum, concert style.

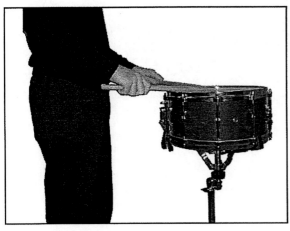

Stands: It is important for the surface of the batter head to be approximately waist high. This enables the percussionist to use the proper technique and encourages good posture. Adjustable stands for concert usage need an easy height adjustment mechanism as well as a sturdy base. Most importantly, they need to go high enough! Drum set stands are not recommended for concert use.

Stance: When standing, the player's feet should be slightly apart, weight distributed evenly, the batter head at waist level and the snare release facing the player. Any music stand is normally placed on the opposite side of the drum, so that the player, drum, stand and conductor are in a straight line.

Sticks: Drum sticks come in a great variety of sizes, styles and weights. Many brands use a number/letter system to help you select the appropriate size. A light, thin stick may be needed for very young children with small hands. Otherwise, select a standard concert weight pair of sticks.

Grips: Using an identical snare drum grip for both right and left hands (the matched grip) will take less time to master. Grips for timpani sticks and mallet-keyboard instruments are similar. When holding any stick or mallet, use only enough pressure to keep it from slipping.

Matched Grip: Grasp the snare stick about one third the distance from the butt end using the thumb and index finger. The thumb should be parallel to the shaft, pointing toward the tip of the stick. The index finger is crooked around the stick which lies diagonally across the palm. Wrap the other three fingers lightly around the stick and turn the hand so that the knuckles are facing up.

Traditional Grip. The right hand is the same as above. For the left hand, the stick is placed in the well of the thumb about one third the distance from the butt end. The ring and little fingers are crooked underneath the stick, which rests on the ring finger. The index and middle fingers curl lightly over the stick. If it is necessary to use the traditional grip in the left hand, you will need to make sure the playing surface of the drum or practice pad is at the appropriate angle.

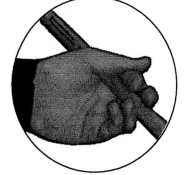

Playing Area/Tone Production: The general playing area on the snare drum is just off center, away from the player (toward the music stand). The tips of the sticks should fall within an area no larger than a half dollar to insure creating an identical sound with both left and right hands. The player can use the surface of the drum to help control the dynamic level by moving the tips of the sticks toward the rim of the drum to achieve a softer sound and toward the center for louder dynamics. It is important that the snares always speak and that the drum's tone is resonant, yet crisp.

Basic Motions: There are a variety of approaches to striking the drum. Whichever one is used, the action should be relaxed and natural. Avoid tension!

Arm Stroke: This basic action involves the arm, wrist and hand in a smooth, coordinated motion. The elbow moves away from the body as the relaxed wrist and hand rise above the drum. On the downward motion, the action is rapid and is sometimes described as "snapping a whip", or "flicking water from your finger tips". After the stick strikes the drum, it is allowed to bounce or 'rebound' freely to create a full, resonant tone.

Wrist Stroke: This basic action involves primarily the wrist and hand. The stick is raised high above the drum head by the wrist alone. Its action is sometimes pictured as 'waving goodbye'. Again the stick strikes the drum and is allowed to rebound freely, creating a full, resonant tone.

Rebound Strokes: (single & multiple)

  Single rebounds: Taking advantage of the flexing surface of the drum, the player can use the natural rebound of the stick to play rapid reiterations. Controlling the stroke's rebound so that the stick rises just a few inches from the drum head surface and is allowed to fall back once, and only once, is called a *single rebound* stroke. It is used to play fast, repeated notes in figures such as *paradiddles* and the *open roll*. It is very difficult for beginning drummers to control a rebounding stroke action. To begin with, practice the *single rebound* stroke slowly at a loud dynamic level.

  Multiple rebounds: Allowing the stick to rebound more than once is the stroke action used to create the *closed,* or *concert-style* roll. After striking the drum, allow the stick to bounce freely, like a ball, until the action stops. Learning to control this action takes less time than the single rebound approach and its use is recommended as part of a beginning approach to playing closed rolls.

Notation: Snare drum notation includes a variety of traditional music symbols as well as unique ones. Even though the sound of the snare drum is short, composers traditionally use the same rhythmic notation for the snare drum that is used for all other instruments. When playing single strokes with an ensemble, the rhythmic figures are usually the same for the snare drum. Half notes, whole notes, etc. are used so that the snare drummer can count and phrase the same as the rest of the ensemble. What is unique to the snare drum are notations used to indicate a sustained sound, i.e., *the roll*. Composers use two main ways to notate snare drum rolls: (1) three slashes; or (2) "tr", the sign for tremolo. It is important for a snare drummer to be able to interpret both notations.

Sticking: *Idiomatic patterns*: Many of our snare drum rhythmic patterns come from the military tradition. As the snare drummer marched, the swing of the drum against the leg helped dictate sticking patterns. A list of drum rudiments is included with this manual as a reference source, as beginning players will find most of the patterns too difficult. Onomatopoetic terms such as paradiddle and rata-ma-cue help the player memorize both the rhythm and its sticking. As you will see, the stickings used for each rhythmic figure give the patterns their unique feel, or rhythmic flow.

Sticking Policy: For the most part, snare drum sticking is usually designed to enhance the ebb and flow of the music. Just as a violinist uses up and down bowing motions to correspond with weak and strong beats, the snare drummer uses left and right hands to do the same. Sometimes rapid tempi or difficult rhythmic patterns make this approach impossible and a more expedient sticking is used. Students who have a clear understanding of the need for stickings that correspond to the music and who practice often-used snare drum patterns will play more musically and become better sight-readers.

Snare Drum

Warm-ups

Siwe

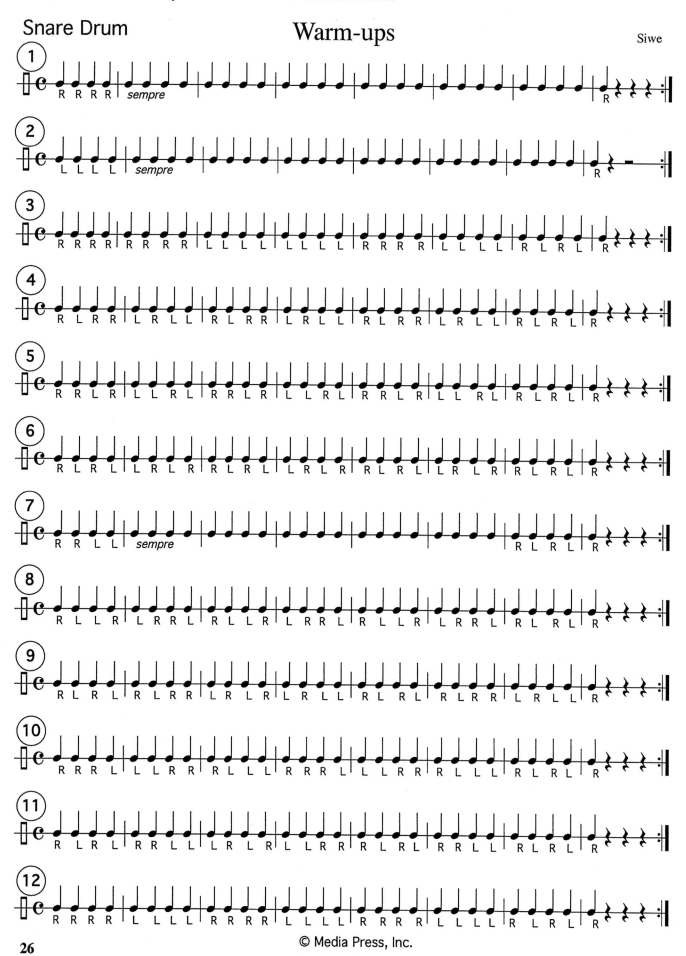

26

Sticking Patterns-Quarter Notes

Siwe

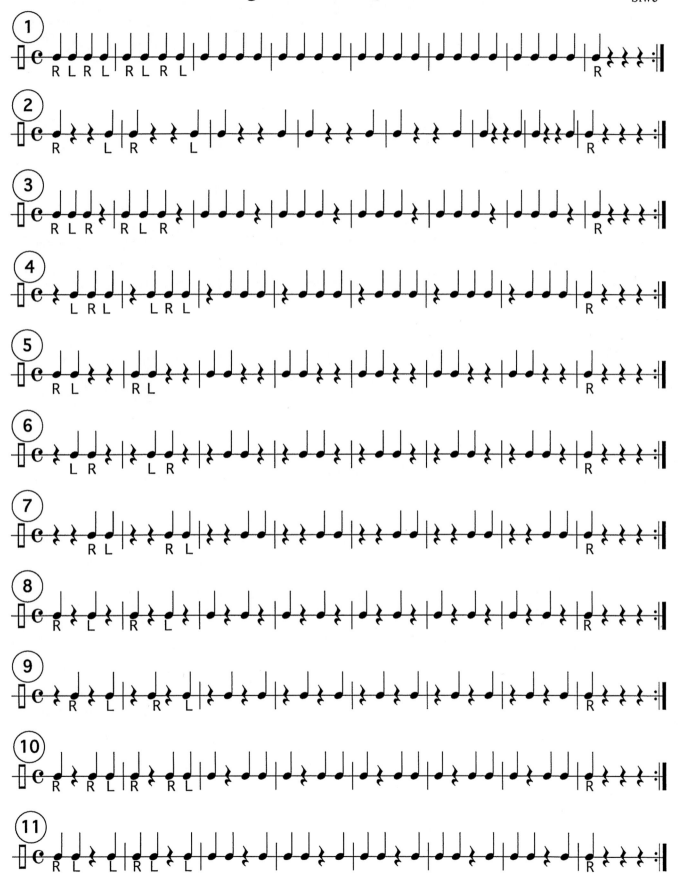

Solo No. 1

(quarter notes)

Siwe

Snare Drum

Sticking Patterns-Eighth Notes

Siwe

Solo No. 2

(eighth notes)

Siwe

Sticking Patterns - Sixteenth Notes

Siwe

Solo No. 3

(sixteenth notes)

Siwe

Sticking Patterns in 6/8

Siwe

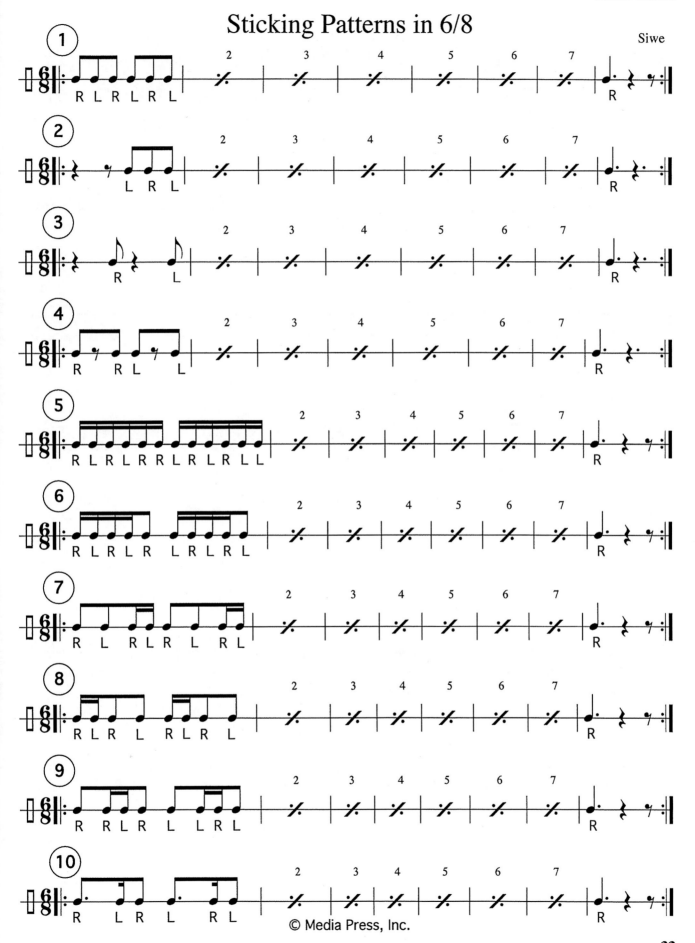

Solo No. 4
(in 6/8 time)

Siwe

© Media Press, Inc.

MULTIPLE-BOUNCE ROLL EXERCISES

Siwe

Ex. I

Ex. 2

Ex. 3

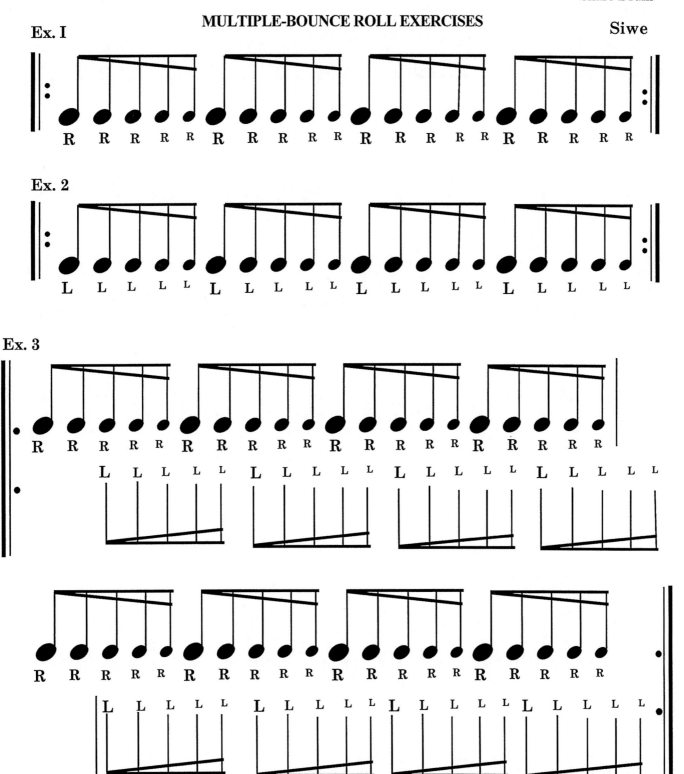

Practice these three exercises very slowly, M.M. = about 40 beats to each beam grouping. Allow your sticks to bounce at least 5 notes or more per group. As your metronome speed increases the amount of strokes per grouping will decrease; never use less than three bounces per group. Try various dynamic levels. The end goal is a smooth, even roll.

Snare Drum # Roll Development Exercises Siwe

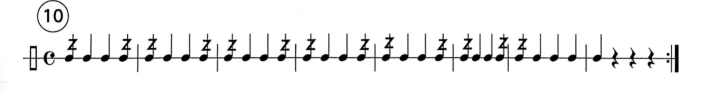

5-Stroke Roll

Siwe

Open Version

Closed Version   (**Z** = multi-bounce stroke)

Practice closed version of the 5-stroke roll slowly, using a metronome.

As your speed increases, the number of multiple bounces will decrease.
Don't use less than three bounces per stroke!

Be sure to play the non-rolled notes cleanly, allowing the stick strike the drum no more than once.

When you feel confident, try the exercises below starting slowly and working toward 120 beats to the quarter note.

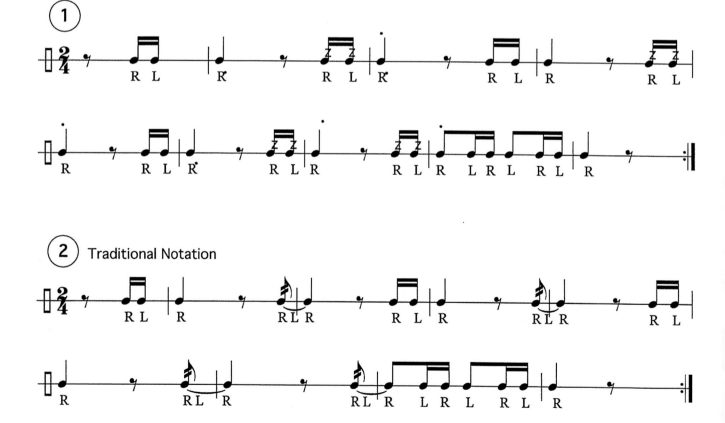

①

② Traditional Notation

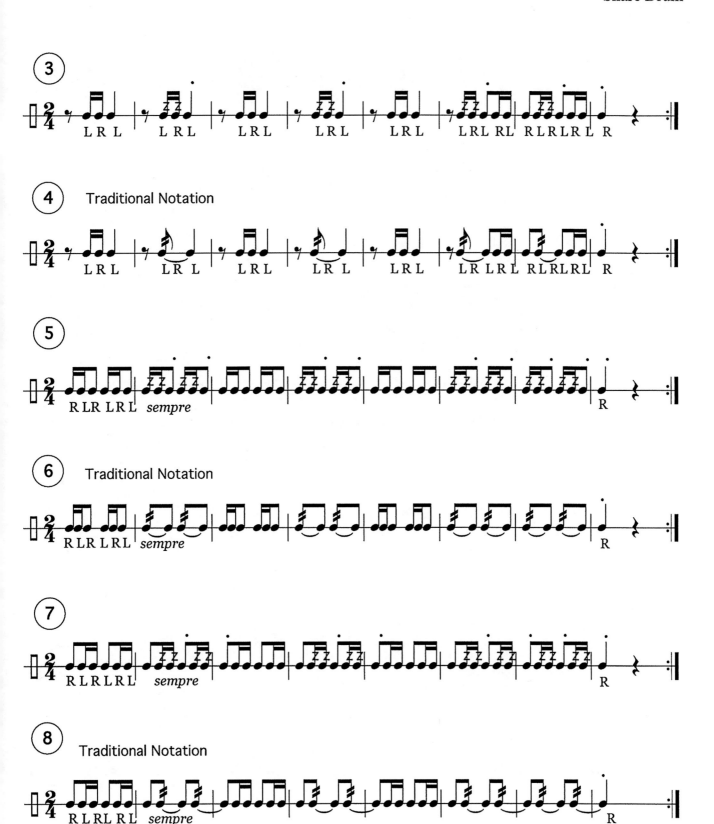

7-Stroke Roll

Siwe

Open Version

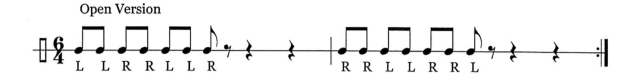

L L L R R L L R   R R L L R R L

Closed Version (Z = multi-bounce stroke)

L   R   L   R   R   L   R   L

Practice closed version of 7-stroke roll slowly, using a metronome.

As your speed increases, the number of multiple bounces will decrease.
Don't use less than three bounces per stroke.

Be sure to play the non-rolled notes cleanly, allowing the stick to strike the drum no more than once.

When you feel confident, try the exercises below starting slowly and working toward 120 beats to the quarter note.

① R   L R L   *sempre*   R   L

② **Traditional Notation**

R   L R L   *sempre*   R   L

Snare Drum

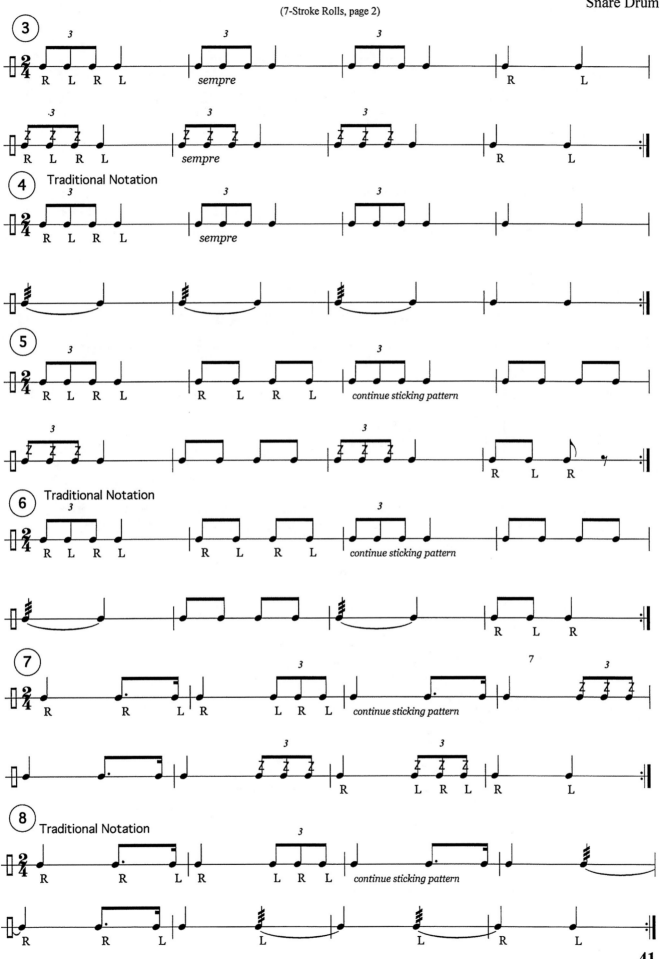

9-Stroke Roll

Siwe

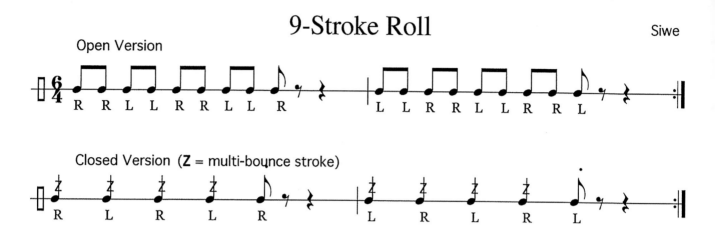

Practice closed version of 9-stroke roll slowly, using a metronome.

As your speed increases, the number of multiple bounces per stroke will decrease.
Don't use less than three bounces per stroke.

Be sure to play the non-rolled notes cleanly, allowing the stick to strike the drum no more than once.

When you feel confident, try the exercises below starting slowly and working toward
120 beats to the quarter note.

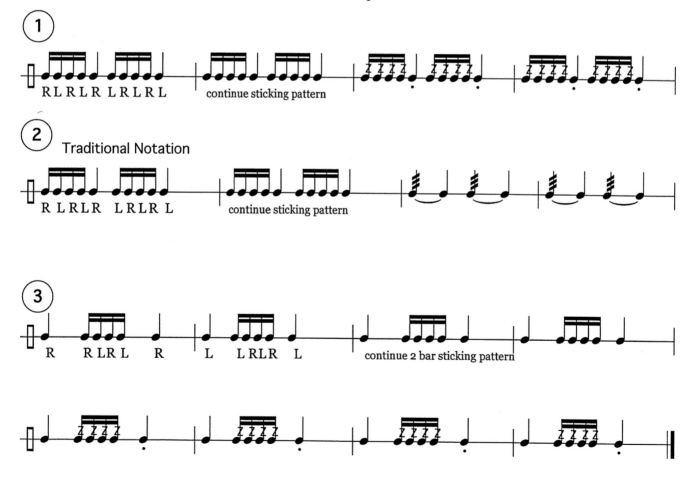

(9-Stroke Roll, p. 2)

13-Stroke Roll

Siwe

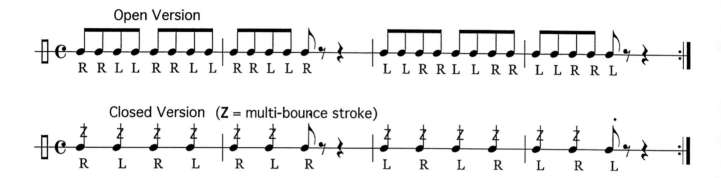

Open Version

R R L L R R L L R R L L R

L L R R L L R R L L R R L

Closed Version (**Z** = multi-bounce stroke)

R L R L R L R

L R L R L R L

Practice closed version of 13-stroke roll slowly, using a metronome.

As your speed increases, the number of multiple bounces per stroke will decrease.
Don't use less than three bounces per stroke.

Be sure to play the non-rolled notes cleanly, allowing the stick to strike the drum no more than once.

When you feel confident, try the following exercises starting slowly and
working toward 120 beats to the quarter note.

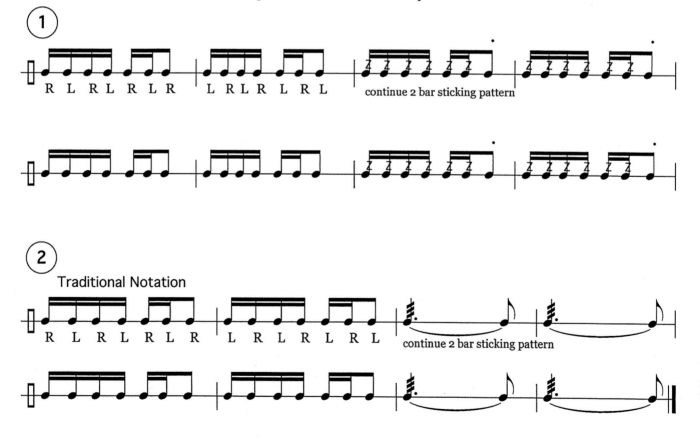

①

R L R L R L R   L R L R L R L   continue 2 bar sticking pattern

②

Traditional Notation

R L R L R L R   L R L R L R L   continue 2 bar sticking pattern

(13-Stroke Roll, p. 2)

17-Stroke Roll

Siwe

Open Version

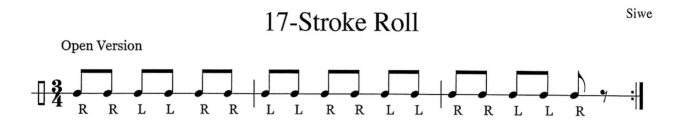

Closed Version (**Z** = multi-bounce stroke)

Practice closed version of 17-stroke roll slowly, using a metronome.

As your speed increases, the number of multiple bounces per stroke will decrease.
Don't use less than three bounces per stroke.

Be sure to play the non-rolled notes cleanly, allowing the stick to strike the drum no more than once.

When you feel confident, try the following exercises starting slowly and
working toward 120 beats to the quarter note.

1

repeat 2 bar sticking pattern

2

repeat 2 bar sticking pattern

17-Stroke Roll, p. 2)

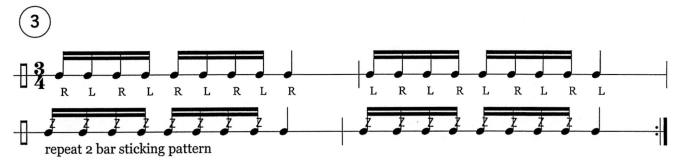

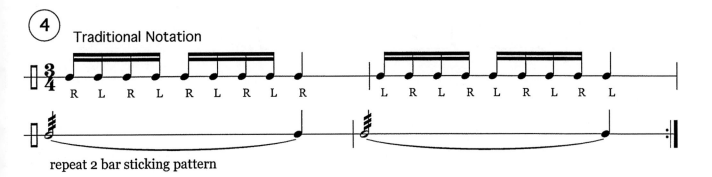

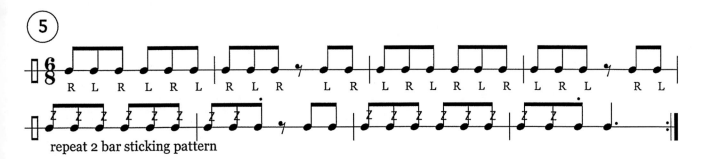

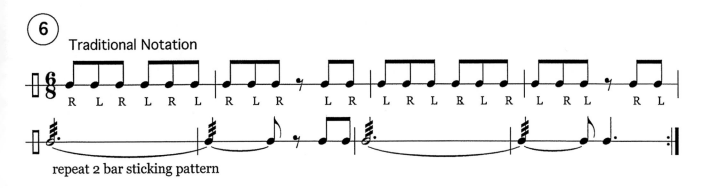

Snare Drum

Cadence No. 1
(5-stroke rolls)

Siwe

Cadence No. 2
(5-stroke rolls)

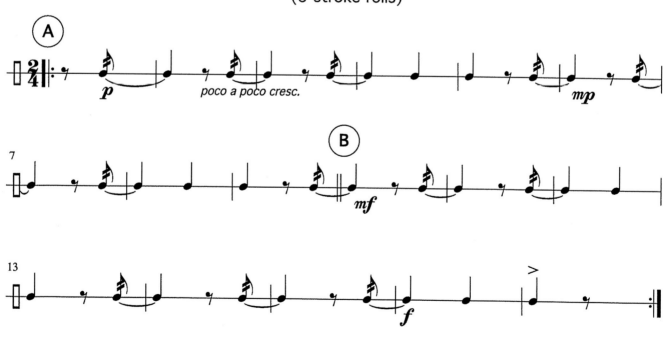

Snare Drum

Cadence No. 3
(5-stroke rolls)

Siwe

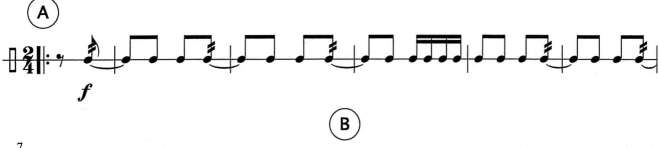

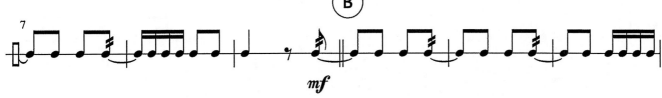

Cadence No.4
(5-stroke rolls)

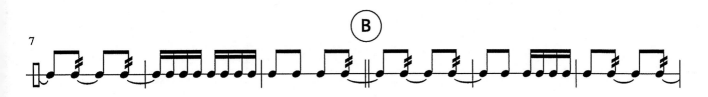

Snare Drum

Cadence No. 5
(7-stroke rolls)

Siwe

Cadence No. 6
(7-stroke rolls)

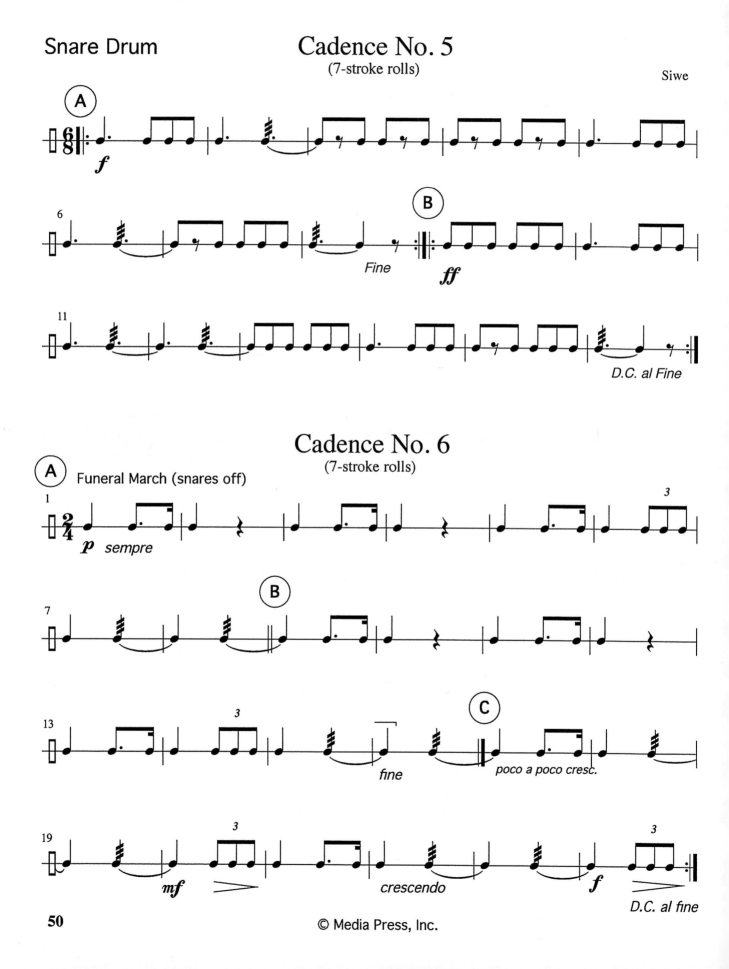

Cadence No. 7

(9-Stroke Rolls)

Snare Drum

Siwe

Cadence No. 8

(13-Stroke Rolls)

March Tempo

Snare Drum

Cadence No. 9
(with 13-Stroke Rolls)

Siwe

© Media Press, Inc.

Cadence No. 10

(17-Stroke Rolls)

Snare Drum

Siwe

5-Stroke Etude
(with 5-Stroke Rolls)

Snare Drum

Siwe

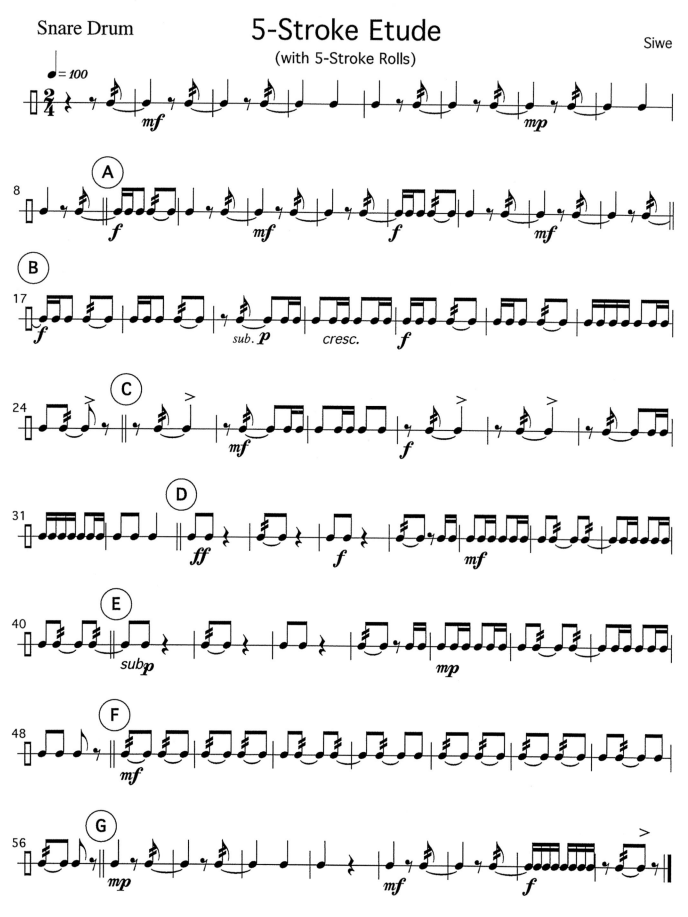

7-Stroke Etude

(with 7-Stroke Rolls)

Snare Drum

Siwe

Snare Drum
9-Stroke Etude
Siwe

(with 5- and 9-Stroke Rolls)

13-Stroke Etude

(with 7- and 13-Stroke Rolls)

© Media Press

13-Stroke Etude II

Siwe

(with 5-Stroke, 9-Stroke and 13-Stroke RollS)

Snare Drum

17-Stroke Etude

(with 5-Stroke, 7-Stroke, 13-Stroke and 17-Stroke Rolls,
introducing the 'rim shot' and 'on the rim.')

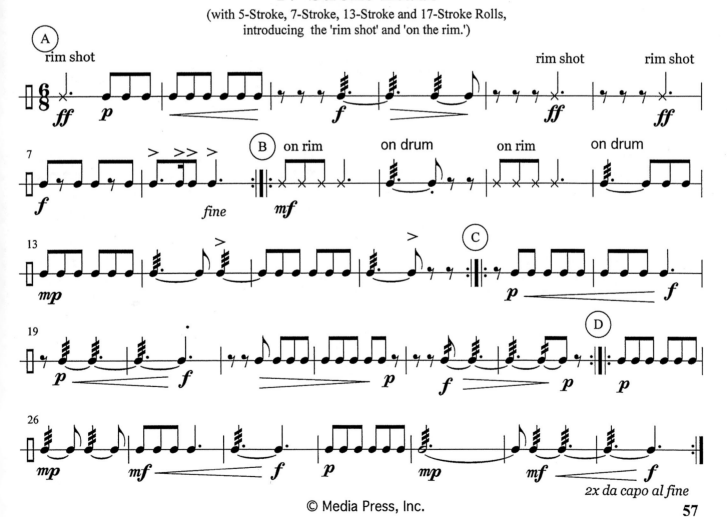

Snare Drum 17-Stroke Etude II

Siwe

(with 5-Stroke, 9-Stroke, 13-Stroke and 17-Stroke Rolls)

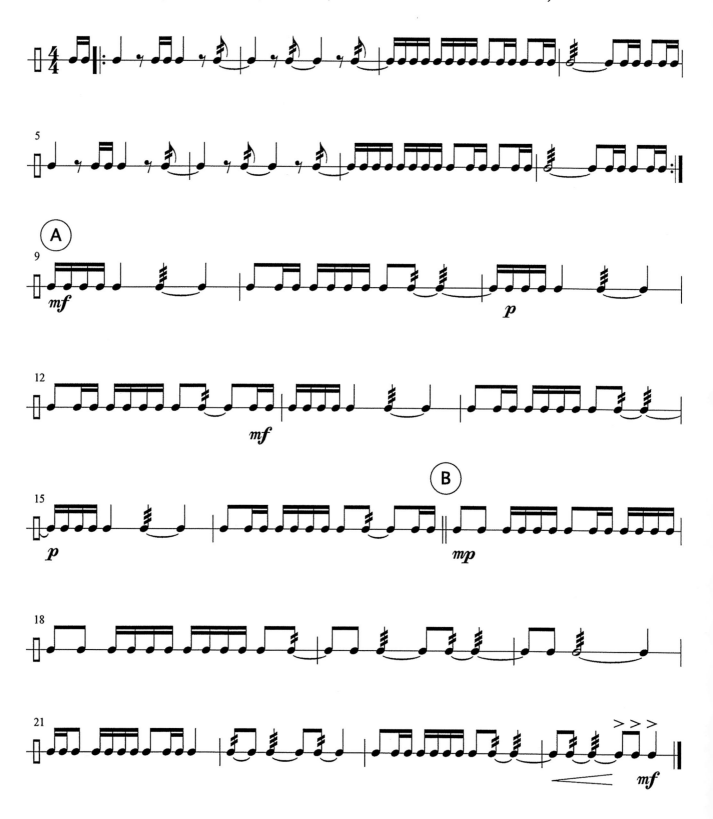

© Media Press, Inc.

Flams

(single grace notes)

For the snare drum, the "flam" designates a single grace note attached to a larger note. When practicing flams, be sure the larger note falls directly on the beat. The grace note is played just before the larger note and slightly softer, but does not create a 'ta-DAH' sound. Instead, it is a single, composite sound, i.e. like the word 'flam'.

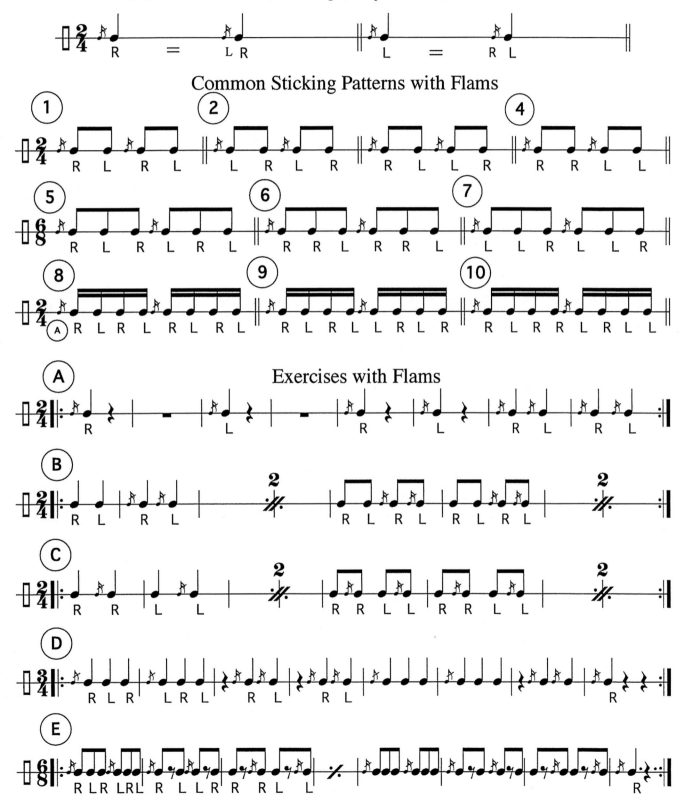

Common Sticking Patterns with Flams

Exercises with Flams

Snare Drum

Flam Cadence No. 1

Siwe

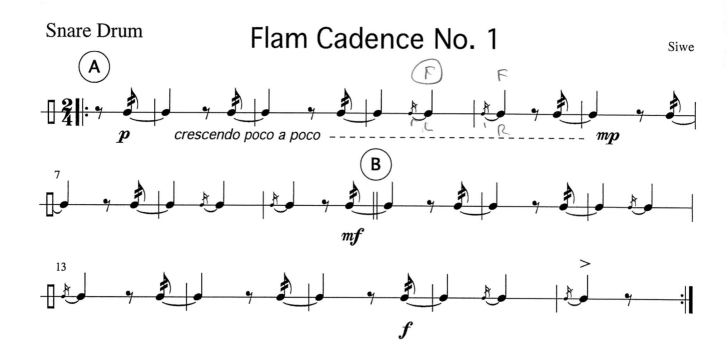

Flam Cadence No. 2

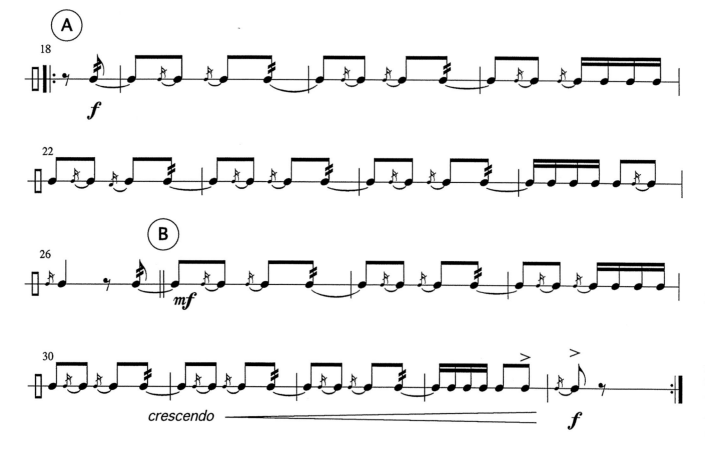

Flam Cadence No. 3

Snare Drum

Siwe

Flam Cadence No. 4

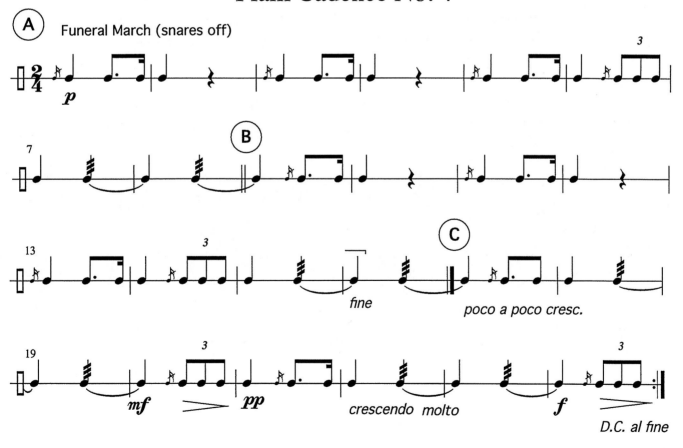

Snare Drum

Flam Etude No. 1

Siwe

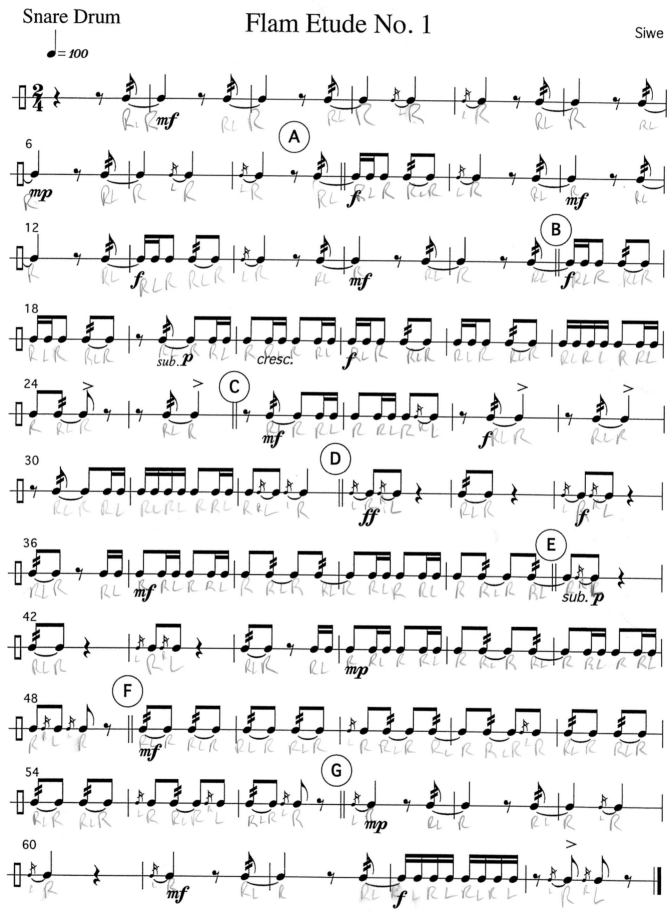

© Media Press, Inc.

Flam Etude No. 2

Snare Drum   Siwe

Drags
(double grace notes)

Drags are notated as two grace notes before a larger note and played either open or closed. For young players, it is easier to first learn the closed style. The grace notes are played with a multi-bounce stroke (more than two strokes) preceding the large, or terminating note. The sound of the closed drag imitates the word 'zump' with the terminating note accented. For open drags, the player controls the rebounded grace notes so as to cleanly articulate them both. In each version, open and closed, the larger or terminating note falls directly on the beat at a louder dynamic than the grace notes.

Common Sticking Patterns with Drags

Exercises with Drags

Drag Cadence

Snare Drum

Siwe

Ruffs

"Ruffs" are notated for the snare drum as a series of two or more grace notes (usually not more that five) followed by a terminating note. They are always articulated, either by employing alternate sticking, i.e. L-R-L-R etc., or by controlling the rebound so that only the correct amount of notes sound. Ruffs are very difficult for beginning players to execute. Composers tend to notate ruffs at cadence points, or in support of an accented figure, not always giving the player ample time to prepare. As with flams and drags, the terminating note falls directly on the beat and is given a slight accent.

Exercises To Develop 4-Stroke Ruffs

Snare Drum

Ruff Cadence

Siwe

Rim Shot Etude

Siwe

Snare Drum

© Media Press, Inc.

Bass Drum

History: A hollowed log with skin coverings on both ends was probably the Bronze Age version of our contemporary bass drum. "Surprisingly, perhaps, one of the most familiar of the drums of to-day [sic] and an instrument by no means unknown in ancient times, the 'bass drum', seems to have had little or no place in Europe in the Middle Ages or the Renaissance." (Blades 1970, 205). The bass drum was definitely used in the nineteenth century orchestras of Beethoven and Haydn, though probably with a wider shell and a smaller head diameter. Today's bass drum sizes range from a small twenty-inch drum set model to the colossal eight foot show drums found in a few marching bands. The modern corps style marching bass drum and the concert hall version have little in common today except the name. A calfskin-headed drum that provides a low booming sound of indefinite pitch is the standard for concert usage, while the drum corps bass drum has evolved into a choir of drums with plastic heads and a penetrating, focused sound easily heard out-of-doors.

Construction and Nomenclature

Bass drums are constructed with wooden shells and, like snare drums, have heads on both sides. The heads are mounted on wooden or metal hoops (flesh hoops) and have sufficient slack, or 'collar', so that the drum can be tuned. The tuning rods have 't-handles' to facilitate tuning, which must be done often with calf skin heads. Again, like the snare drum, it is important to apply tension evenly at each tuning post. Calf skin heads are recommended for their quality of sound, but using plastic heads may be more practical for younger players. Plastic heads are always used for outdoor performances. The air hole on a bass drum can cause problems since small objects can be inserted into the drum through the hole causing unwanted rattling. A small piece of window screen duct-taped firmly to the inside will help prevent this problem.

Sticks

The size and weight of bass drum mallets will, to a large extent, determine the sound produced. For general playing, use a large, heavy, felt covered mallet. For rapid passages played with a full tone, use one of a pair of general purpose rolling sticks. Additional mallets of use are: light-weight rolling mallets, extra-large cartwheel timpani style sticks, and a double headed mallet for one-handed rolls.

Grips

Bass drum mallets are held using the matched grip. The thumb is placed parallel to the shaft at a point of balance with the remaining fingers wrapped loosely around. When playing rolls, the bass drum should be tilted at an angle that assists the player's arm motion or laid flat.

Stance/Dampening

To play the concert bass drum in an upright position, the player stands behind the drum, slightly to the playing side. One knee is used to help control the head resonance on the playing side of the drum, while the opposite side head is controlled by placing one's hand on it as needed. The drum can be played at an angle or laid flat; tilting stands will help facilitate this. In the flat position, the bass drummer must find ways to help control the drum's resonance. The use of a cloth, or small bath towel, positioned on the head will reduce the resonance, producing more defined, rhythmic articulations. Dampening with the free hand will also help control the drum.

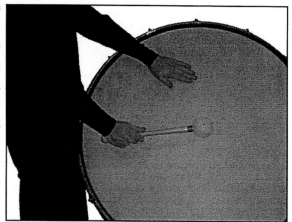

Sizes

Concert bass drums range in size from fourteen-inch to eighteen-inch shell diameters. The smaller diameter shells may be easier for young people to use since it is necessary when playing to place one hand on each side of the drum. The head diameters range from twenty-eight to forty inches in diameter. Remember, the larger the drum, the lower the pitch.

Stands

A tilting bass drum stand provides the greatest flexibility of use. Bass drum stands that tilt come in two models: suspended or non-suspended. The former offers the greatest resonance, but is the most difficult to control. Both models have wheels that make moving the drum easier. A folding portable model stand is also used today, though it is unsteady and often produces unwanted rattles.

Tuning

Each bass drum head is tuned evenly from post to post so that it resonates freely, without any 'flapping' sound. When tuned properly, it should produce a low 'boom' sound with no identifiable pitch or unwanted overtone.

Playing Area/ Tone Production

As the diagram on the next page shows, the bass drum has three distinct tonal areas. For general playing, use the area just off the center. Try slightly different playing spots to get the articulation and sound quality desired. The area directly in the center will produce the shortest duration and most muffled quality. It is used for 'cannon shots'. Near the edge of the head the sound quality 'thins', but it makes soft rolls easy to produce.

Rolls

Bass drum rolls required two mallets of the same size. Place each mallet opposite one another away f rom the drum head center to produce the fullest sound possible. Use a single stroke roll similar to the timpani roll.

Stroke

For a fundamental sound and best control, the bass drum stroke should be a smooth arm and wrist motion. The stroke moves directly into the drum and rebounds back to the desired height. The breadth and force of the motion determine the dynamic, a larger motion will produce louder notes, while keeping the mallet close to the head will produce a softer sound. Avoid glancing blows and 'dead' strokes.

Notation

Bass drum notation is similar to that of the snare drum. Sustained sounds (rolls) use both the slash notation and the 'tr' (tremolo) notation. Since the sound of the bass drum can continue for a great deal of time after the drum is struck, many composers carefully notate the exact duration wanted; others do not. It is up to the percussionist to listen carefully to the other musicians and determine when to dampen and when to allow the drum to resonate.

Sticking

Since bass drum parts are most often played with one hand only, sticking is not a great concern. Observing accents, both written and natural, is an important part of playing the drum. When two mallets or sticks are used, the player observes the same rules that apply to sticking snare drum passages.

Bass Drum Playing Areas

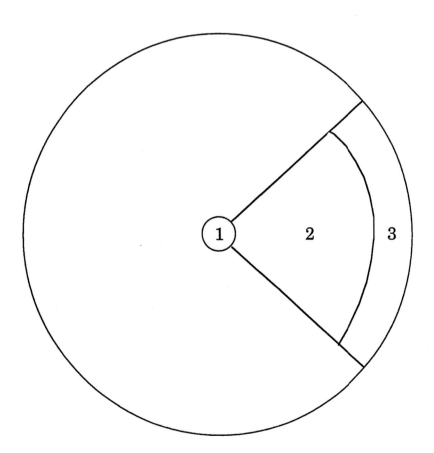

1. Secco (cannon shot) 2. General Playing Area 3. Soft rolls, special effects

Etude for Solo Bass Drum

Siwe

Cadence No. 1

Bass Drum

Siwe

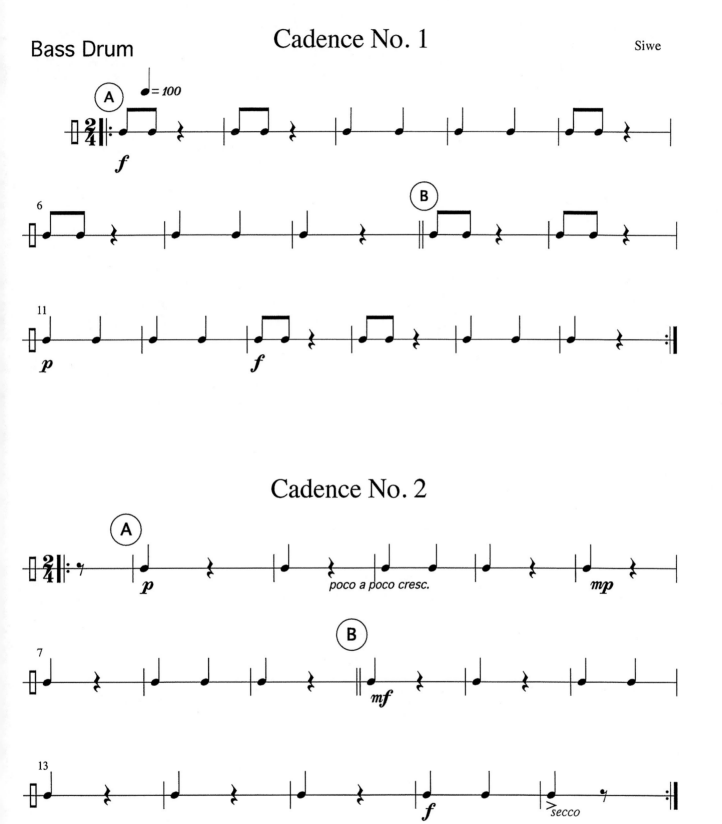

Cadence No. 2

Bass Drum

Cadence No. 3

Siwe

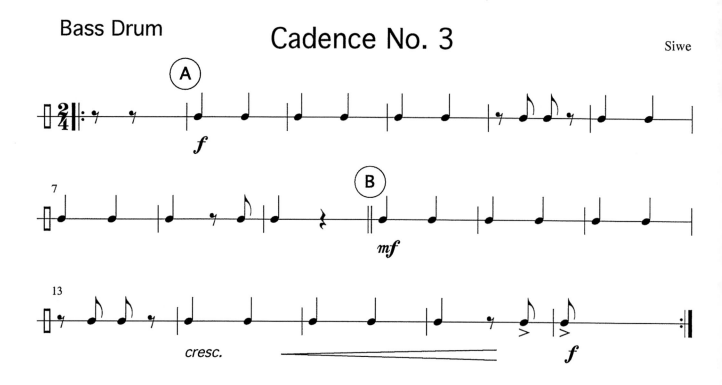

Cadence No. 4

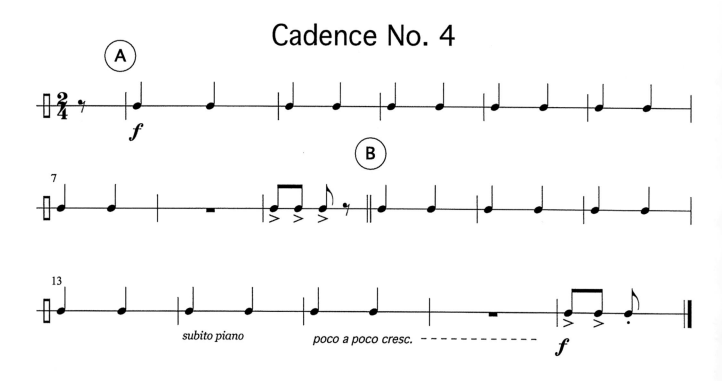

Cadence No. 5

Siwe

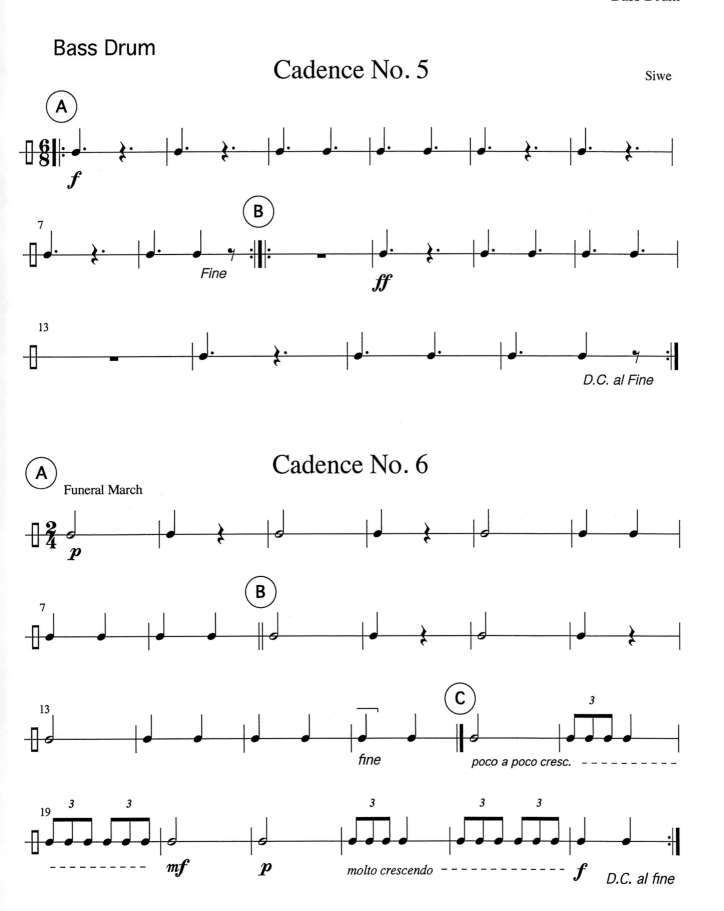

Cadence No. 6

Cadence No. 7

Siwe

Bass Drum

Cadence No. 8

March Tempo

© Media Press, Inc.

Bass Drum

Cadence No. 9

Siwe

Cadence No. 10

2x d.c. al fine

Bass Drum

5-Stroke Etude

Siwe

© Media Press, Inc.

Bass Drum

7-Stroke Etude

Siwe

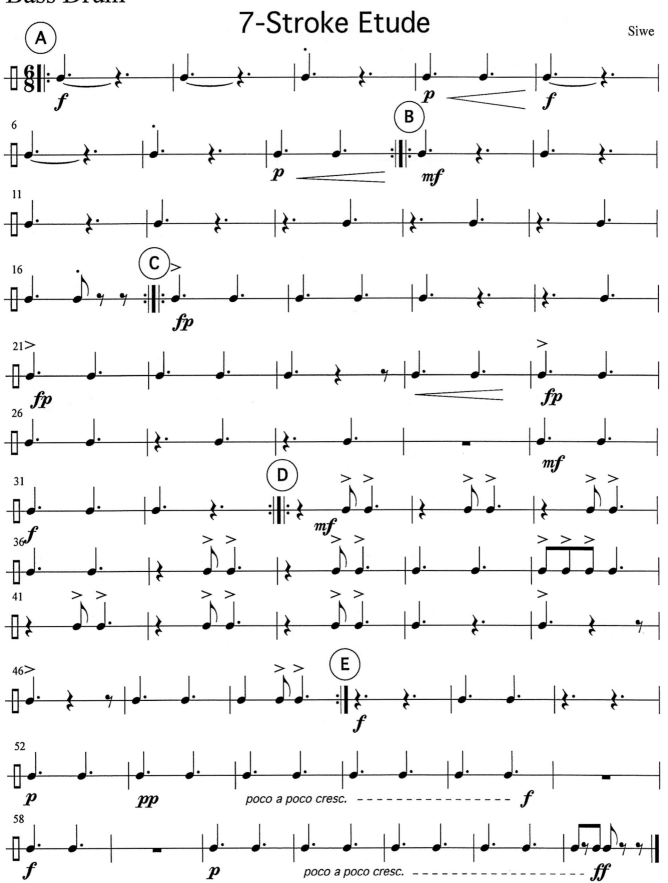

Bass Drum

9-Stroke Etude

Siwe

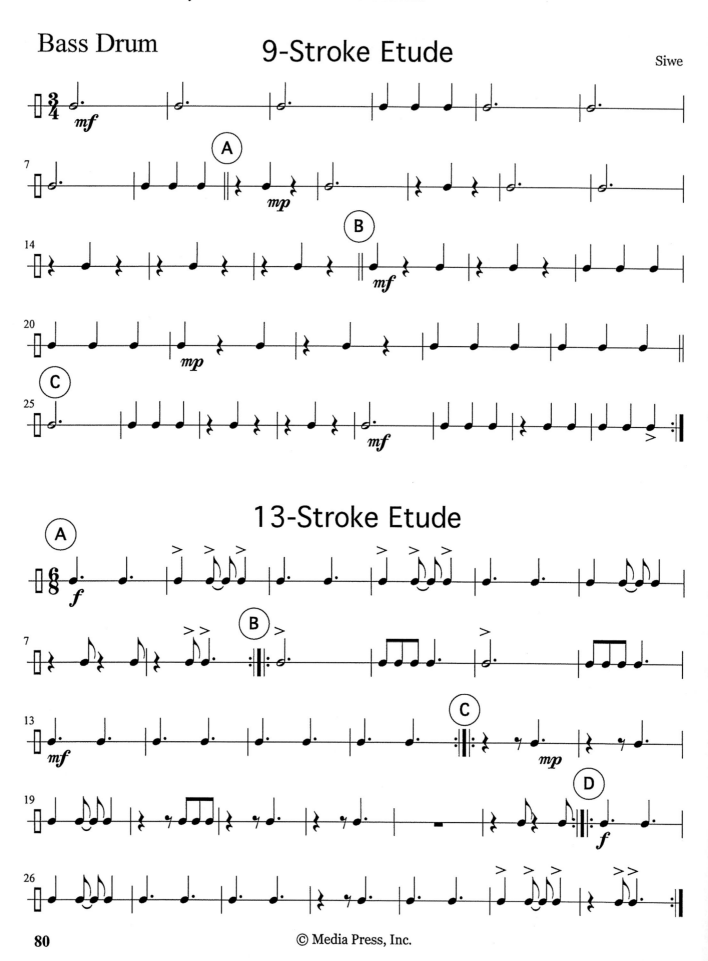

13-Stroke Etude

Bass Drum

13-Stroke Etude II

Siwe

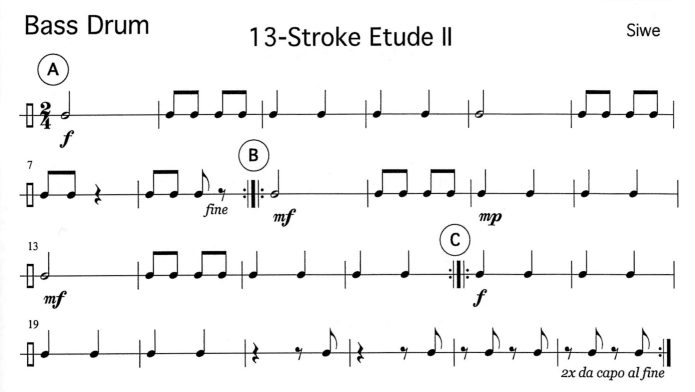

17-Stroke Etude

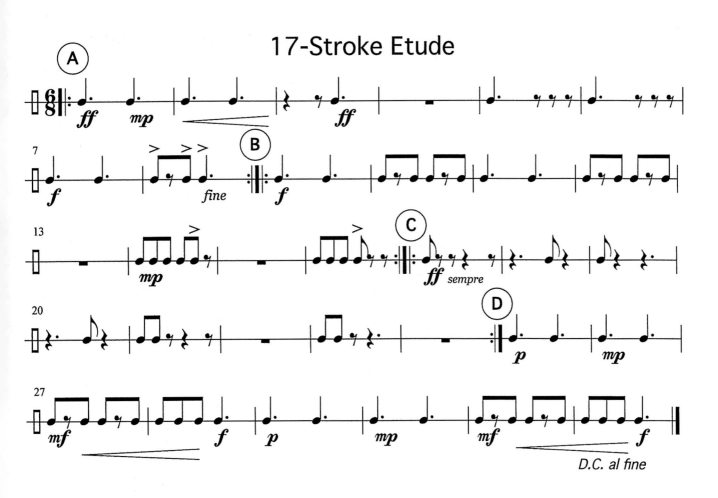

Bass Drum

17-Stroke Etude II

Siwe

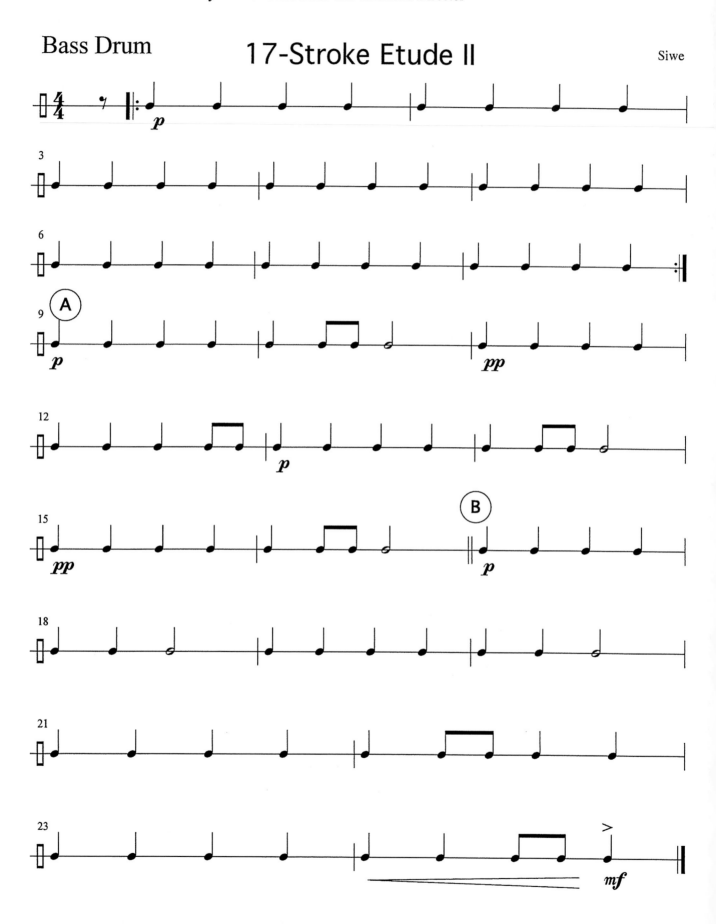

Cymbals

bell · bow · edge

History

Cymbals have a documented history of over 2,000 years. They "were in use in Israel by ca. 1100 B.C." (Marcuse 1964, 137) and other Middle East countries, depicted on many tombs and temples and chronicled in a number of Old Testament books. In the beginning their role was "ritual rather than martial" (Marcuse 1964, 138). At the time of the Moor's invasion of Spain in 694, cymbals were part of military bands, and later, along with drums, triangles and Turkish crescents, comprised the percussion section of the elite Janissary bands of the sultan's guard during the Crusades. Their orchestra debut did not occur until the late 17th c. (N. A. Strungk's opera *Esther*, 1680). The "Turkish Music" craze of the late 18th c. established the use of cymbals in the orchestra and opera through works by Haydn, Mozart and Beethoven

Cymbals are made of a bronze alloy consisting of roughly eight parts of copper to two parts of tin with a trace of silver. The craft of making cymbals is carried on today in numerous cultures throughout the world. Contemporary orchestra and band cymbals are available in many styles, sizes and weights.

Nomenclature

As the above diagram shows, each cymbal has three areas: (1) the *bell* (or cup) - a thick, center part of the cymbal with a hole drilled through its middle; (2) the *bow* - a curved and tapered part; and (3) the *edge* - a thin area at the outer circumference.

Selecting cymbals

Cymbals are of indeterminate pitch (owing to the production of inharmonic partials). When selecting cymbals in pairs for concert use, listen for the following: (1) lack of any strong fundamental pitch; (2) a plurality and balance of overtones; (3) resonance and long decay time. The best way to hear the sound is to activate the entire cymbal by striking it against a flat surface (e.g. the floor or a wooden table).

Each individual cymbal (though difficult to hear) seems to have a pitch. When selecting a pair, try to match two with an interval of a minor second to a minor third. It is not necessary or desirable to find two with the exact pitch. Suspended cymbals need to respond quickly to a strike with a soft mallet. They should have the same three qualities listed above in addition to a 'shimmering' sound when played with yarn covered mallets.

Weights and Sizes

Music instrument catalogs list cymbals in a great variety of sizes and weights. When selecting cymbals, consider not only the sound needed but the weight and size as well. Cymbals are very heavy. Young players find it difficult to play the cymbals using a proper technique if they are are too heavy or too large to control.

Straps and Pads

For school groups, the recommended straps and pads are made of soft leather. The strap is tied to the cymbal using a cymbal knot (see illustration under Care and Repair - Cymbals). It is important to regularly check that the knot is secure and that the strap is not frayed. After use, the cymbals should be stored in a cymbal bag.

Grip

Place the cymbal strap across the palm of the hand and close the fist around it. The flat of the thumb should be pressed against the leather pad and the strap pulled tight giving the player maximum control of the cymbal's attitude

Stance

Place the feet comfortably apart with the right foot slightly ahead of the left. The players weight must be back on the heels to compensate for the weight of the cymbals.

Keeping Time

Often the cymbal player performs in tandem with the bass drum. The two instruments play a time keeping role, emphasizing the music's pulse, as in marches and dance music. The sustained physical action of playing cymbals for a long period of time can quickly produce fatigue. It is recommended that the player tilt one cymbal so that the underside faces up, helping to support its weight by nestling the elbow into one's body. The other cymbal is held over the fixed plate and the player strikes the latter with an up and down motion, again similar to striking a bass drum. The two rules for crashes apply: (1) the cymbals meet at a small angle; and (2) the edges of the cymbals are slightly off center. This time-keeping technique uses gravity on the player's down-stroke, helping he or she to stay relaxed and avoid fatigue.

Dampening

To dampen the cymbal sound, the player pulls the plates back against the chest, midriff, or shoulders (whatever works best). Cymbals should not be dampened by clashing them together with a 'dead stroke' to keep them from sounding. This technique is used only to imitate the sound of hi-hat cymbals, and then only at soft to moderately loud dynamics.

The Solo Crash

There are a number of different ways to approach clashing two cymbals together to produce a 'solo' crash. In one recommended method, the player holds the cymbals vertically and brings them together with enough force to activate both plates entirely. The player immediately responds to the sound and feel of the cymbals and pulls them apart in the opposite direction. This simple concept applies regardless of what the player does prior to or after the cymbals meet. As with the bass drum, players should avoid glancing motions or sliding strokes.

For young players, having the dominant hand move one cymbal toward the other with the same motion used to strike the bass drum seems to produce better control. Two things to remember are: (1) the cymbals should be at an angle toward one another (see illustration on next page) - the louder the crash, the greater the angle; the softer, the smaller the angle; and (2) the cymbals should be aligned so that the edges do not exactly meet (see illustration) - for louder crashes, use a slightly greater off center position, for pianissimo crashes the cymbals are almost exactly parallel. By observing these two rules, the player will avoid an air lock and its resultant poor sound.

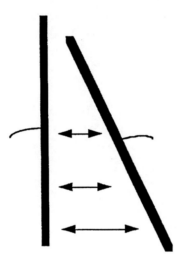

To play a solo cymbal crash, hold the cymbals close together at a slight angle with one cymbal slightly lower than the other. As the graphic indicates, be sure not to slide or slash one cymbal against the other, but bring them <u>directly</u> together with sufficient force to activate both plates. At the moment of impact reverse your arm motions to pull the plates apart so that they resonate freely.

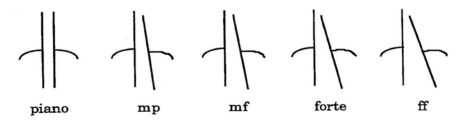

piano   mp   mf   forte   ff

Suspended Cymbal

A single cymbal with a strap can be suspended from a 'goose neck' stand or, without a strap, placed on a cymbal floor stand. Depending on the musical needs, select the appropriate size and weight of suspended cymbal. In general, a 16 inch medium thin cymbal will give a high, shimmering sound. This size and weight cymbal is very effective for soft rolls and accents. For louder, more dramatic musical needs select a larger (18" - 20") medium weight cymbal. Remember that cymbals have an upper dynamic limit and striking (or clashing) them with additional force than needed will only create a distorted sound and may damage the cymbal.

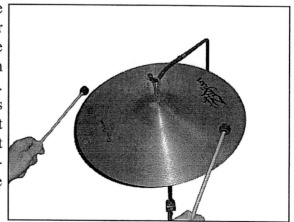

Single notes and rolls
Using a pair of yarn or cord-wound mallets, normally used on marimbas and vibraphones, the player strikes the cymbal on opposite sides of the plate near its edges. Employing both mallets for single notes as well as rolls insures a full tone and good control.

Forte/piano rolls
To produce a forte/piano roll, the player strikes the cymbal and waits a few seconds before starting to roll. Allows the vibrations to dissipate until the desired dynamic level. Then begin to roll, continuing the sound as indicated.

Dampening technique
The sound of the cymbal is dampened by grasping it with the fingers and the fleshy part of the palm making sure the mallet shaft does not accidently make a clicking noise.

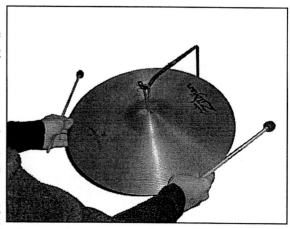

Special effects produced on the suspended cymbal are endless. Composers have explored using the suspended cymbal in many different musical settings and, in so doing, have produced some of the most original notations and symbols. Striking the bell, bow or edge with everything from knitting needles to wire brushes, composers have demonstrated that the suspended cymbal can produce many evocative sounds and subtle variations in timbre.

Etude for Solo Cymbals

Siwe

Slow Waltz Tempo (→ = scrape)

Cymbals

Cadence No. 1

Siwe

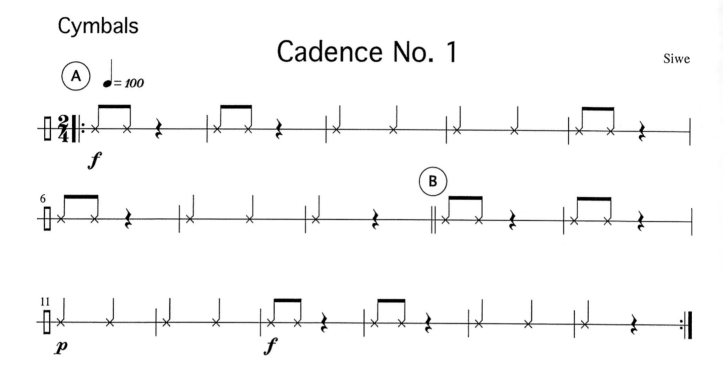

Cadence No. 2

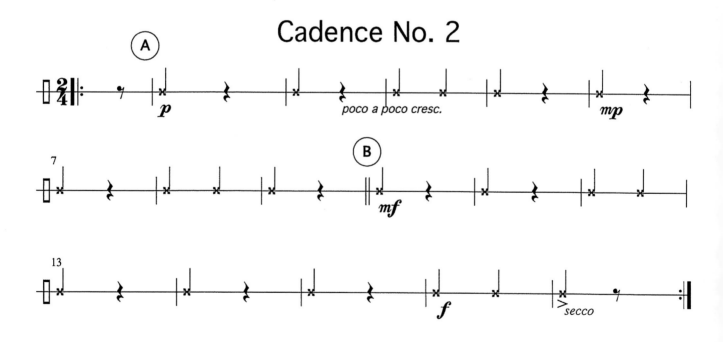

Cadence No. 3

Cymbals

Siwe

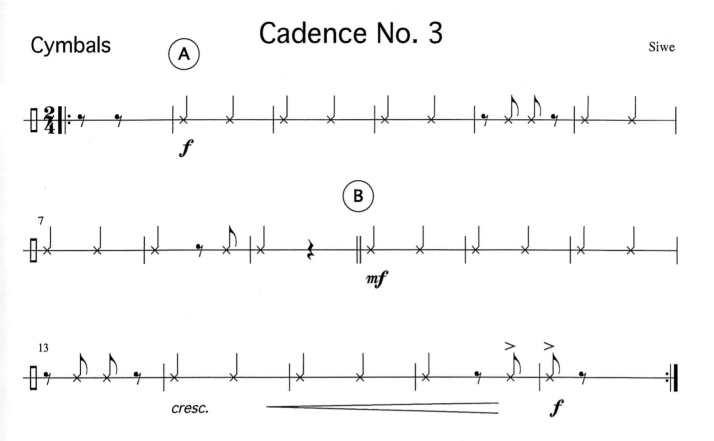

Cadence No. 4

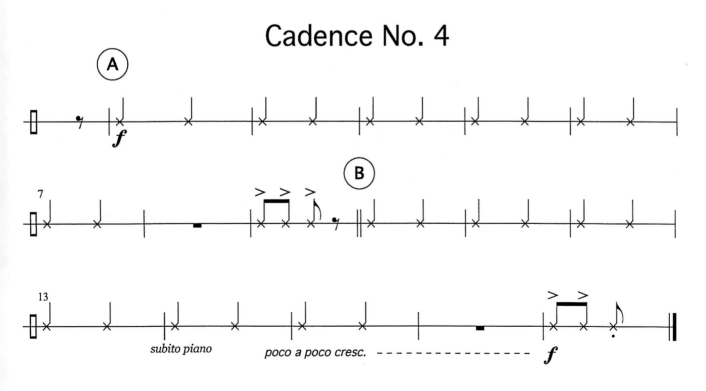

Cymbals

Cadence No. 5

Siwe

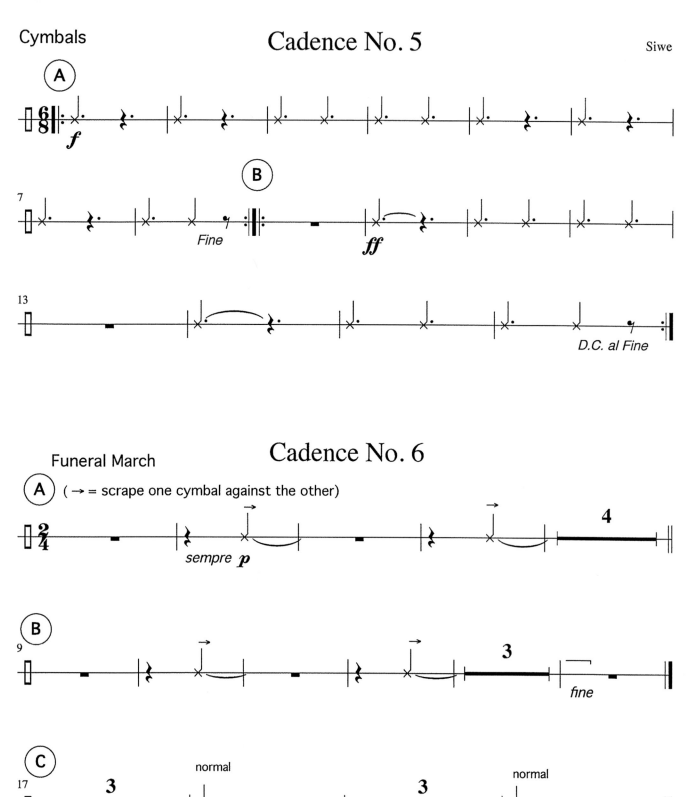

Cadence No. 6

Funeral March

Cymbals

Cadence No. 7

Siwe

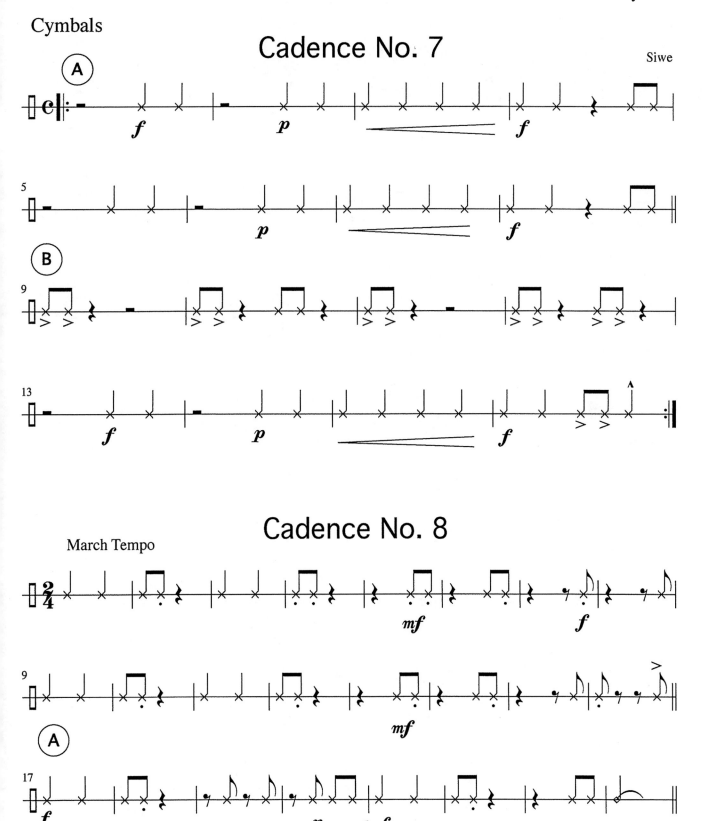

Cadence No. 8

March Tempo

Cymbals

Cadence No. 9

Siwe

Cadence No. 10

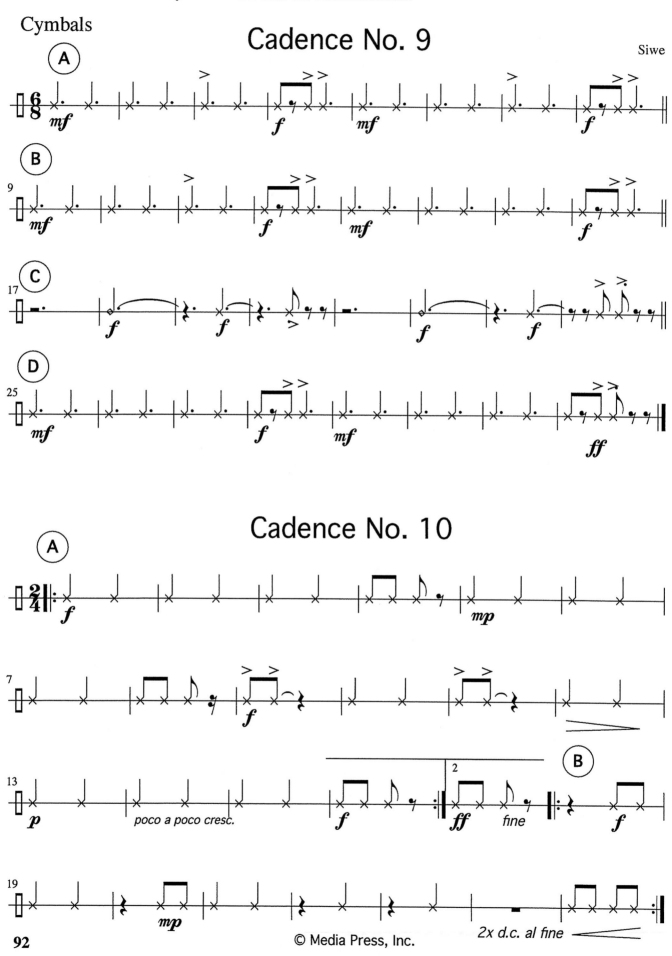

5-Stroke Etude

Siwe

Cymbals

Cymbals

7-Stroke Etude

Siwe

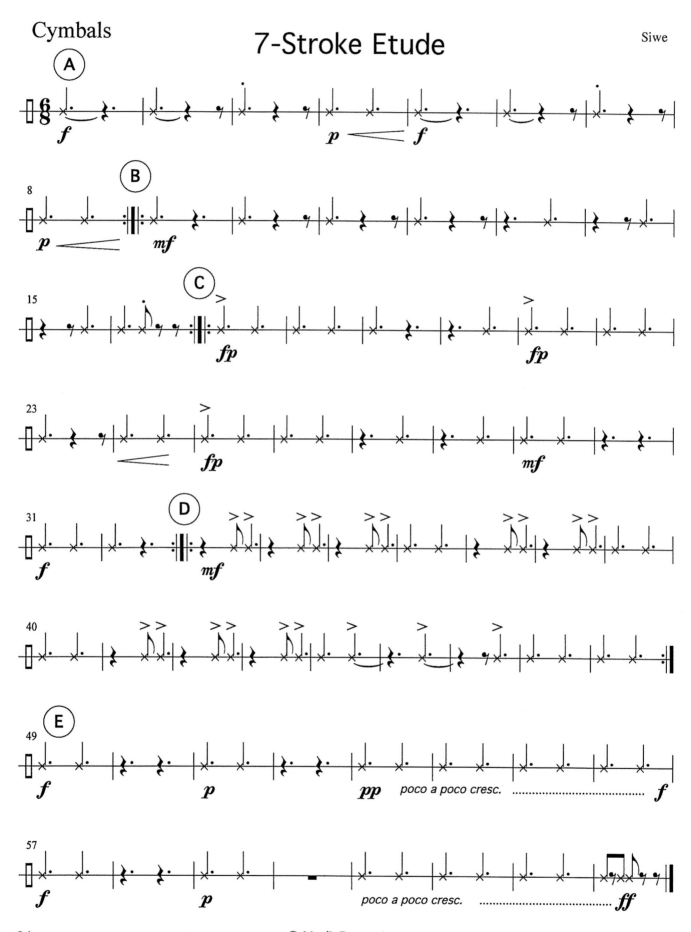

© MediaPress, Inc.

9-Stroke Etude

Siwe

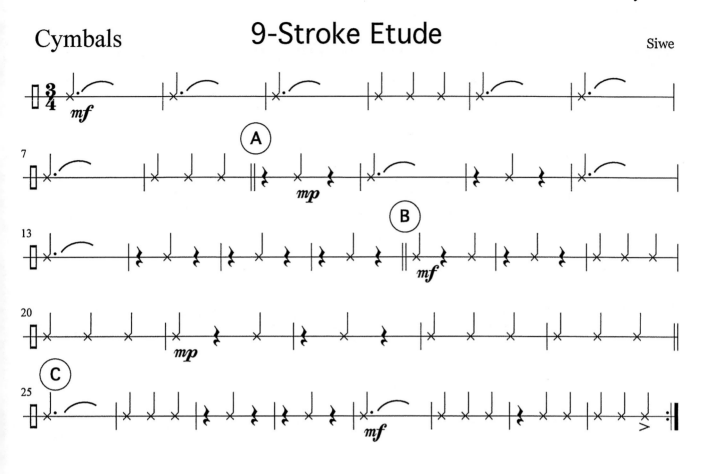

13-Stroke Etude

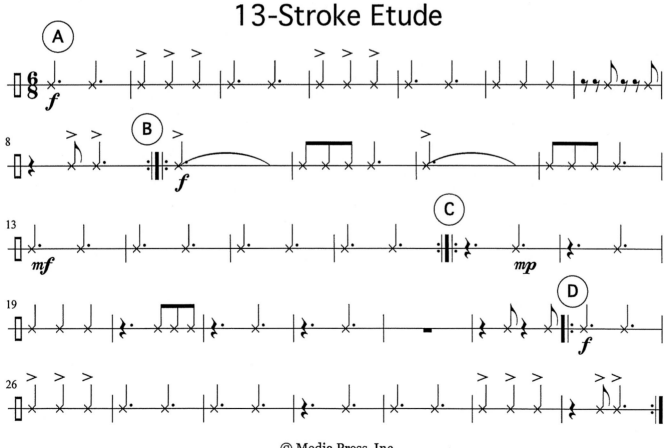

Cymbals

13-Stroke Etude II

Siwe

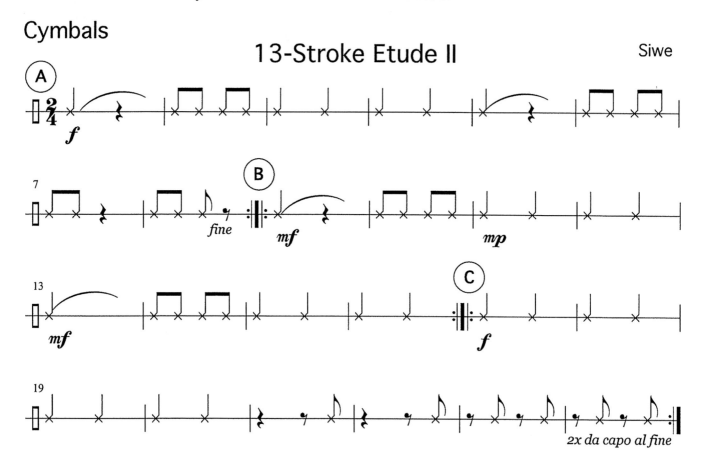

17-Stroke Etude

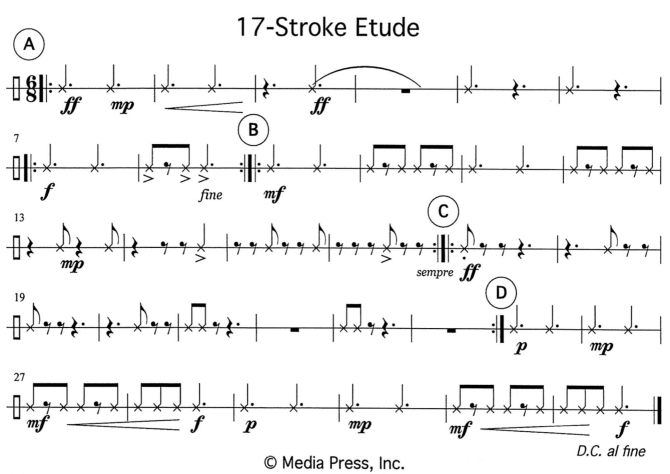

Cymbals
17-Stroke Etude II

Siwe

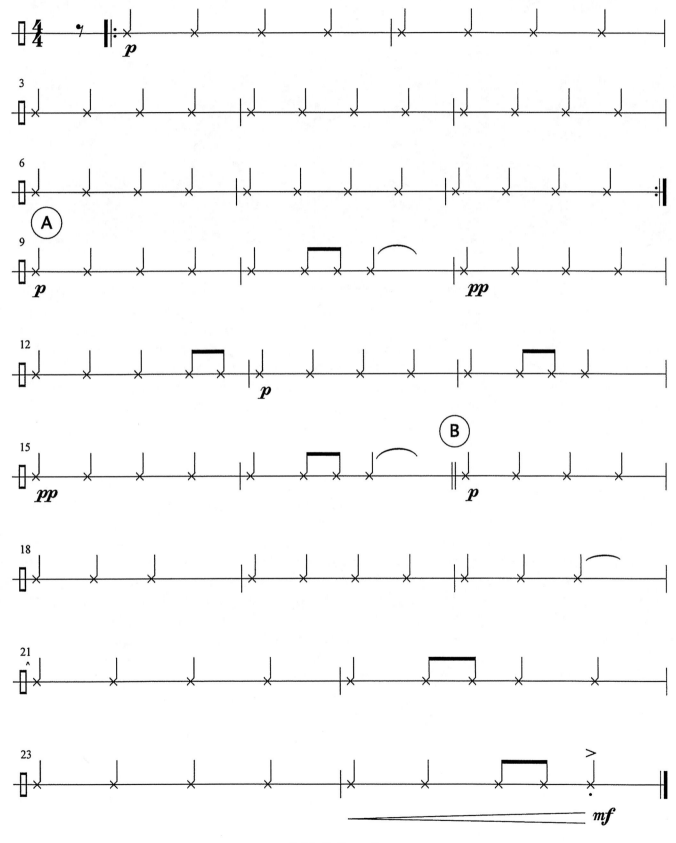

Timpani

History

From the earliest of times, writers have distinguished between timpani (nakers) and snare drums (tabours). Always depicted as single-headed drums with more or less hemispherical resonators, the timpani evolved over centuries to become part of the percussion family of instruments. Used early on to accompany various forms of musical entertainment, (e.g. dancing, court music, tournaments), the timpani, along with trumpets, found a home in the military. Pairs of kettledrums mounted on horseback served as early communication devices on the battlefield and provided, along with choirs of trumpets, music for parades and other ceremonial occasions. Capturing an enemies colors and drums was a coup for opposing armies. Through war and trade, timpani found their way into the West and began to be used, along with trumpets, in early opera and symphonic music.

Models, Construction and Nomenclature

Various models of timpani are used today. The instrument preferred by most professionals has the 'bowl' suspended inside a heavy metal frame and includes a ratchet pedal mechanism as well as a fine-tuning device. Most school models are lighter in weight, utilizing a plain pedal with a spring-balance mechanism. The bowl is either suspended or fixed in a metal frame which consists of a heavy metal base with struts and linkage devices. The modern timpano has wheels or casters to provide ease of movement. Its head is held in place much like the snare drum head, with a metal counter-hoop that has six or eight tension rods, or posts, linked to a spider array. This array is attached near the base to the drum's pedal. Pressing forward on the pedal, as you would a car gas pedal, will cause the tension array to pull the counter-hoop down over the bowl, thus tightening the head and raising its pitch. None of this will work well unless the head is tuned correctly, i.e., set to a correct basic pitch with evenly-tensioned posts.

Set of Drums

A standard set of timpani consists of four drums that are defined by the head diameter, i.e. 32 inch, 29 inch, 26 inch, and 23 inch. Each drum has a chromatic range of a perfect 5th (see Tuned Membrane chart). Together the range extends to an octave and one half. The drums are arranged in a semi-circle, close to one another, but not touching so that the player can easily reach the pedals. An adjustable stool is provided (even though the player may opt to stand when playing) making it possible to place both feet on the pedals at once should the occasion arise.

Mallets/Sticks

Timpani sticks, or mallets, come in a great variety of styles to meet every musical situation. A basic set of mallets for a student would consist of three pairs: one general, one staccato and one wood. The wood sticks are useful for practicing rolls on snare drums pads as well as in musical situations that call for them, saving the more expensive, felt-covered mallets from excessive wear.

Playing Areas/Stroke Actions

Strike each timpano between the two posts directly over the pedal about 3-4 inches from the rim. This impact area is the same when using two, three, or four drums. The player should aim for a single 'beating' spot on the drum head to insure that the pitch and sound quality produced is consistently the same. The player strikes the 'beating' spot moving from drum to drum with the mallet head tracing a smooth arc. Balance and body position are crucial to insure the player has full control over the outside drums.

The basic timpani stroke uses the natural rebound of the drum's head. A combination of wrist and finger action drives the mallet head toward the drum. The louder the dynamic, the longer the stroke; the softer the sound, the shorter the stroke. At the moment of impact, the player stops the downward force allowing the mallet head to rebound naturally. For both timpani grips, the fingers play a crucial roll. They are used extensively to control the force and rapidity of any stroke action. The player's arms and shoulders are used to the extent that is needed to move from drum to drum.

Matched Grip
(aka German style)

Thumbs Up
(aka French style)

Grips

Two basic grips are commonly used by timpanists, i.e. the 'matched grip' (aka German) and the 'thumbs up' (aka French). Unlike the snare grip, the timpani mallet is held quite near the end with the thumb placed parallel to the shaft and the fingers wrapped loosely around with the thumb and index finger opposite one another forming the fulcrum. For 'matched grip' the knuckles face upward; for the 'French' the thumbs are up and the knuckles toward the side. Either grip is acceptable.

Tuning

Ear training is the most important aspect of a timpanist's training. Students should spend as much time developing their ear as all the other timpani techniques combined. To tune a drum, beginning players use a pitch pipe. As they progress to learning intervals, especially, fourths and fifths, a tuning fork (Bb or A) is used. The player brings his or her head close to the drum, identifies the pitch and with a 'flick of the finger' softly activates the drum head, glissing up to the the desired note. It is important that the technique used to activate the drum results in a true basic sound being produced. A light finger tap will create only high

frequency partials and not the basic pitch. Pressing the finger into the drum before flicking the finger tip forward will help produce the fundamental pitch. Some players softly tap the timpano with a stick, but this can often times lead to the sound being heard as part of the music.

Tuning gauges have now become standard on new drums. They are very useful for making rapid pitch changes and changes within the context of a work. Keeping the gauges in adjustment takes great care and can be part of the young timpanist's training.

Dampening and Mutes

To dampen the timpani sound, place the finger tips on the head near the impact area. Be careful not to create an unwanted sound. Sometimes the palms are used as well, especially at the louder dynamics. It is a standard procedure to dampen the drums in rhythm on any rests if the tempo allows. Dampen not only the last drum struck but all those that are still resonating.

Timpani heads are very resonant. To insure that they do not create unwanted sounds when not in use, it is necessary to place mutes on the drums. A circle of felt placed just off the center serves well. These mutes can be used discretely to assist with articulation problems. Moving them near the drum's edge will produce a shorter sound without adversely effecting the tone quality.

Notation

Rolls: Notation for a sustained sound, or roll, is usually indicated by three slanted slashes across a note. Some composers use the *trem.* or *tr.* (tremolo and trill symbols) and/or a wavy line. Beginning the roll, the timpanist gives the drum a clear stroke so that the sound is immediately heard. If the roll ends in a terminating note, the drum is again struck cleanly on the beginning of the beat. For rolls that have no terminating note, the sound is dampened at the very last beat subdivision, or as the music dictates.

Single Notes: The duration of single strokes is not always clearly notated. Composers often use the most convenient rhythmic notation and leave the articulation and dampening to the timpanist's discretion.

Forte-piano Rolls: To execute a forte-piano roll, the player sharply strikes the timpano with one mallet. When the drum decays to the piano level, the player quickly begins a soft roll. This is a popular device with which composers sometimes begin crescendos.

Sticking

It is important for young players to learn to use both right and left hands and to move easily from drum to drum. Rhythmic passages are played by alternating hands. To move from one drum to another, the player must decide which hand is best to begin with so that the need to cross over is minimized. Composers rarely indicate sticking. It is up to the player to clearly mark stickings in the part.

Tuned Membranes

Siwe

Timpani

(timpano - singular)

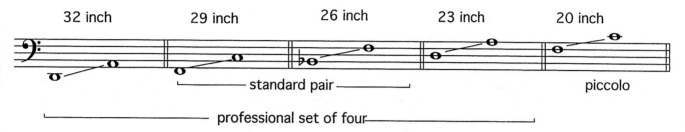

Rototoms

(timp-toms)

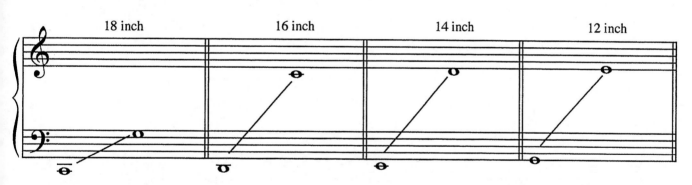

Stands are presently designed to hold any two drums, or the three small drums as a set.

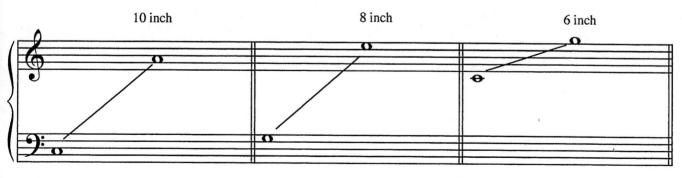

Timpani Roll Development

Siwe

(Timpani Roll Development, p. 2)

Timpani Scale Etudes

Siwe

Etude for Low Drum

Etude for High Drum

Etude for High and Low Drums

Timpani Interval Etudes

Siwe

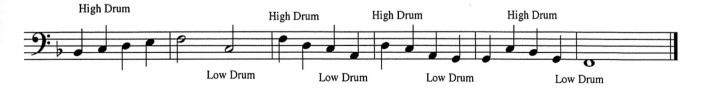

Timpani Test Pieces

Siwe

No. 1

poco a poco cresc.

Timpani Test Pieces

Siwe

No. 2

Timpani

Cadence No. 1

Siwe

Cadence No. 2

Timpani

Cadence No. 3

Siwe

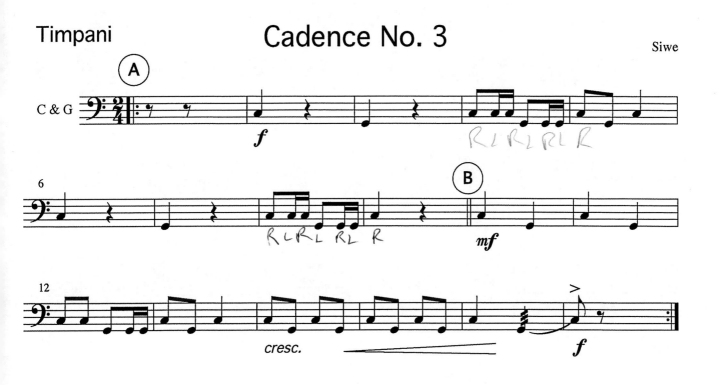

Cadence No. 4

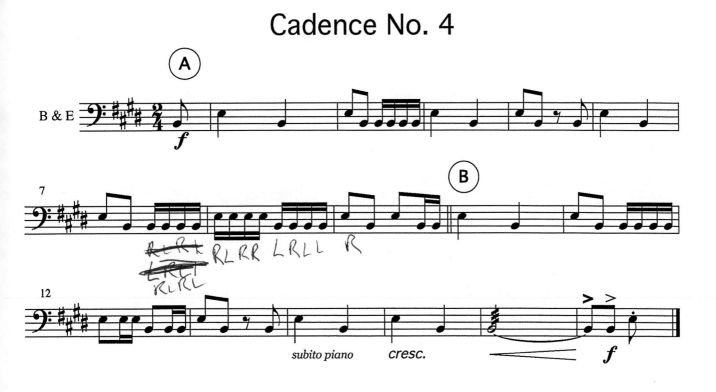

Timpani

Cadence No. 5

Siwe

Cadence No. 6

Funeral March

Cadence No. 7

Timpani

Siwe

Timpani

Cadence No. 8

Siwe

Cadence No. 9

Timpani

Siwe

Timpani

Cadence No. 10

Siwe

2x d.c. al fine

5-Stroke Etude

Timpani

Siwe

7-Stroke Etude

Timpani

Siwe

9-Stroke Etude

Siwe

13-Stroke Etude

Siwe

Timpani

13-Stroke Etude II

Siwe

2x da capo al fine

Timpani

17-Stroke Etude

Siwe

2x d.c. al fine

17-Stroke Etude II

Timpani

Siwe

Triangle

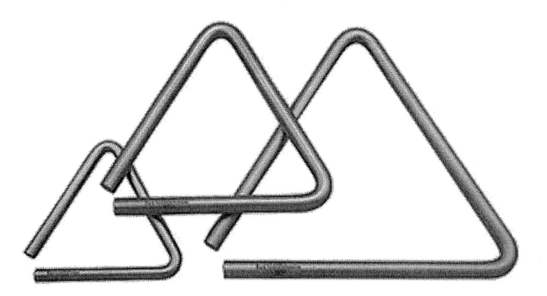

History

"The triangle, named for its shape, was closely allied in one of its medieval forms (with rings strung to the lower bar) to the ancient sistrum" (Blades 1970,191). The jingles attached to the base of a triangle, or the bars of the sistrum, created a tambourine-like sound when struck or shaken. Mentioned in the bible and ancient treatises, it appears that both the triangle and sistrum were used in religious services throughout the ages. The sistrum is still used today in the Coptic Church services of northern Africa.

The triangle used by today's percussionists shed its jingles sometime in the 18th century. It found its way into the Classical orchestra of Mozart and Haydn as part of the Janissary music craze (Mozart: *Die Entführung aus dem Serail* (1782); Haydn: *L'incontro improvviso* (1775). By the time of Liszt it had "reached solo status in the Piano Concerto in E-Flat Major (1855)" (Beck 1995, 337).

Today, composers use the triangle as another orchestral color. The desired sound is a high frequency 'tinkle' with a blend of overtones that avoids any sense of definite pitch. Suspended, it is normally struck with a small metal beater, but it can also be hit with wood stick, rattan handle or any hard object. In popular music, it serves as a rhythm instrument. Gripping the triangle on one side, the player squeezes and releases (dampening and opening) the instrument in rhythm while striking with the other hand to create a subtle, rhythmic line.

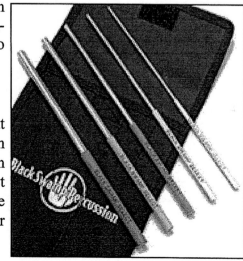

Beaters

Triangle beaters are bought or made in pairs. Basic pairs are cut from steel rod with diameters of 1/16,1/8 or 3/16 by 8 inches in length. Triangle beaters can easily be made from stock found in most hardware stores. It is important to smooth the ends to protect the player's hand. Commercial sets of triangle beaters are available from music stores. The ends are sometimes covered with plastic or rubber tubing and often come with a cloth storage bag.

Holders

Triangle holders, or clips, can be purchased from any music store. They can also be made from metal clamps available in hardware stores or from modified music clips (See illustration Care and Repair - Triangle). Many professional percussionists use a second 'safety' loop of string to insure against the possibility of a break in the primary loop.

Sometimes rapid passages require the player to use two beaters. In this case, suspend the triangle using two clips at the closed corners and attach the instrument to a music stand. Using a pair of beaters, strike the base of the triangle near its middle. Note: Clipping the triangle to a stand changes its sound quality and most players use this procedure only when necessary.

Performance Techniques

Hold the triangle by cupping the hand to form the letter 'C' and inserting the holder with triangle so that the thumb and first or middle fingers support their weight. The remaining fingers can then be used to dampen the triangle sound when needed by closing around its apex. Be sure that the closed end of the triangle faces the hand holding the beater.

The triangle beater is held at its very end with the thumb, first and middle fingers. To perform passages using one beater, strike the triangle on its base near the closed end. To play fast-moving passages, to execute a roll or to perform embellishments use the side nearest the corner and the triangle base. Rapid back and forth motions are easily executed.

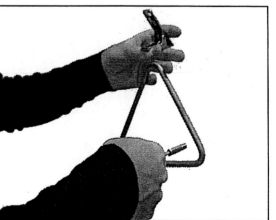

Dynamics are controlled both by the force of the striking motion and the diameter of the beater. The player must choose the best size beater (s) for a given musical passage.

Triangle Exercises

Siwe

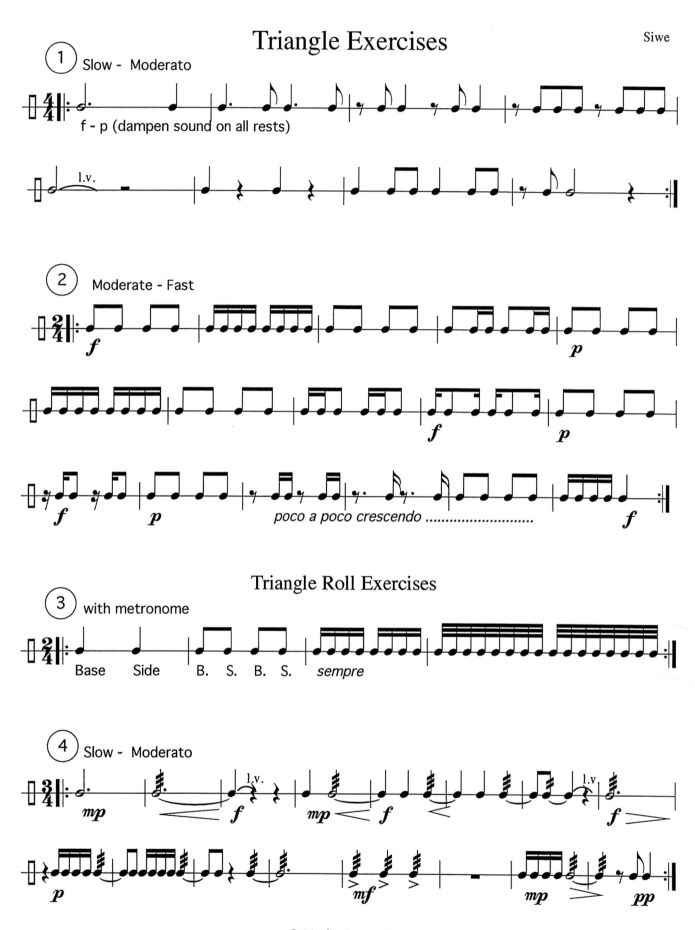

Embellishments

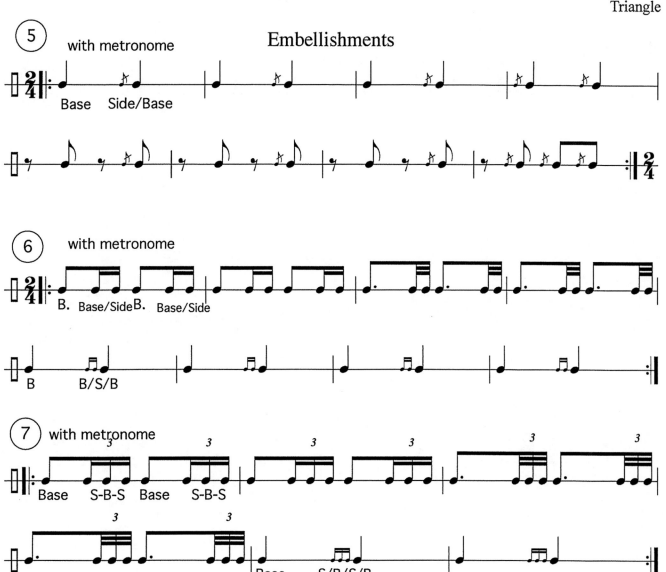

Etude for Triangle

Triangle

Duet for Triangle and Tambourine

Siwe

Waltz

Triangle

Trio for Triangle, Tambourine & Castanets

Siwe

127

Tambourine

History

A hand-held, single-headed frame drum, the tambourine can be classified as either a membranophone or an idiophone, depending how it is played. Its ancestor, the frame drum, has a documented history that predates 20th century B. C. Depicted on reliefs from ancient Egypt and Greece, many versions of the frame drum continue in use today throughout India, the Middle East and the Arctic Circle. Frame drums sometimes have small bells, jingles, metal rings or other rattling elements attached. The drums are used to accompany dances and are played by both men and women. As early as the 18th century, the tambourine appeared in works by Gluck (*Echo et Narcisse* (1779) and Mozart (*German Dances* k 571-1787). Nineteenth century European composers utilized it increasingly in their orchestrations, often to evoke the folk music of gypsies or other ethnic groups. Today, the tambourine is exploited both for its membranic and idiophonic possibilities. A headless version makes a great rhythm instrument for pop and Latin groups.

Sizes/Models

The 10-inch diameter tambourine with a single row of jingles is the most widely used instrument. Smaller instruments and those with double rows of jingles are popular as well. Jingles are formed in diverse patterns and are made from various metal alloys. These variations provide subtle timbre differences described as 'lighter' or 'darker,' 'ringing' or 'dry.'

Grip

A small hole, useful for mounting the tambourine on a stand, is located at the mid-point on the drum's shell. The player carefully picks up the tambourine at this point since it is void of jingles. When moving the instrument, always keep it at a slight angle to minimize the possibility of extraneous rattling sounds. A padded tray stand and a small hand towel (or sponge rubber piece) are useful to insure silence. How the player grasps the instrument depends on the technique employed.

Performance Techniques

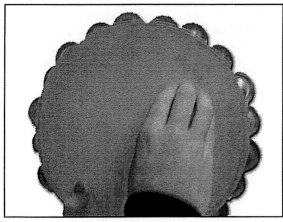

Loud/Slow Passages

Grasp the tambourine with the thumb on the head and the fingers wrapped around the shell. Raise the instrument (keeping the head angled slightly downward) so that it is at eye level. Use the combined finger tips of the other hand to form a striking surface, or form a fist and use the knuckles. Bring the tambourine head and the opposite hand in close proximity just above the head mid-point. With a quick, forceful motion bring the two together so that the jingles and head sound simultaneously. Do not allow the hand to rebound.

Soft/Slow Passages

Grasp the tambourine with the thumb on the head and the fingers wrapped around the shell. Raise the tambourine (keeping it at a slight angle to the floor) so that the head is about waist high. Use the combined finger tips of the other hand to form a striking surface. Bring these finger tips close to the very edge of the head, away from the player, and softly strike the tambourine. Do not allow the fingers to rebound.

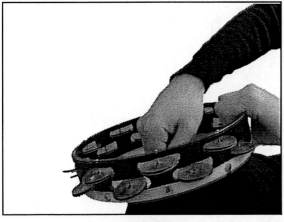

Loud/Fast Passages

Grasp the tambourine with the thumb on the head and the fingers wrapped around the shell. Place your leg on a chair or stool rung. Move the tambourine (keeping it at a slight angle) so that the head is centered just over the knee. With the other hand, combine the finger tips to form a striking surface and center this inside the tambourine opposite your knee. With a forceful wrist action, bring the head down onto the knee and back so that it strikes the other hand. Single-line, rhythmic passages are played using the same right/left
(= knee/hand) approach as for the snare drum

Soft/Fast Passages

Place your leg on a chair or stool rung. Move the tambourine (keeping it at a slight angle) and place it on your thigh, head down, near the knee. Hold it in place with your forearms. Using the fleshy parts of your combined finger tips, softly strike the shell rim. Single line rhythmic passages are played using the same right/left hand approach that determined snare drum sticking.

Rolls

Grasp the tambourine with the thumb on the head and the fingers wrapped around the shell. Raise the instrument (keeping the head angled slightly downward) so that it is at eye level. Strike the head just above the center and rapidly rotate the wrist back and forth. If the notation indicates a terminated note, restrike the head using a dead stroke (no rebound) to stop the sound. If there is no terminating note, simply stop the oscillation and sound by bringing the hand to the head.

Thumb Rolls

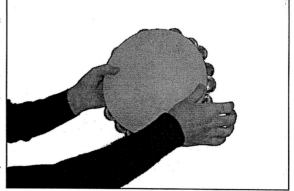

Short rolls are possible using a technique that allows the thumb to scrape across the surface of the tambourine head. Position the tambourine as for playing soft/slow passages. With a light touch, rub the thumb along the outer edge, leading with the tip. Rosin, or similar sticky substance, applied to the rubbing area can be helpful.

Embellishments

Grace notes and other embellishments are played using either the knee/hand or two-handed techniques listed above.

Using Snare Drum Sticks

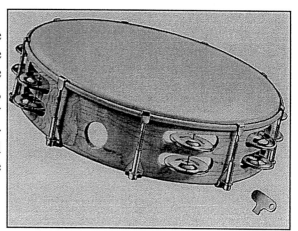

Occasionally a composer calls for the tambourine to be played with snare drum sticks. A plastic-headed tambourine is used for such occasions. It is placed head up on a snare drum stand that can be adjusted to the proper playing height, or it can be placed on a padded surface and angled slightly by placing a towel or sponge rubber piece at one point under the rim. Tunable, plastic-headed tambourines are useful for out-of-doors situations where the humidity cannot be controlled.

Rhythm Tambourines

Headless tambourines are often used in stage bands and combos to add rhythmic background and help keep time. Special tambourines with easy to grip handles are recommended for this purpose. This will help to keep your supply of tambourines used for orchestra and concert band in good repair.

Tambourine Exercises

Siwe

(Tambourine Exercises, p. 2)

Try repeating the final exercise using thumb rolls at mezzo-piano to pianissimo levels.

Etude for Tambourine

Siwe

Tambourine

Duet for Triangle and Tambourine

Siwe

Trio for Triangle, Tambourine & Castanets

Siwe

Tambourine

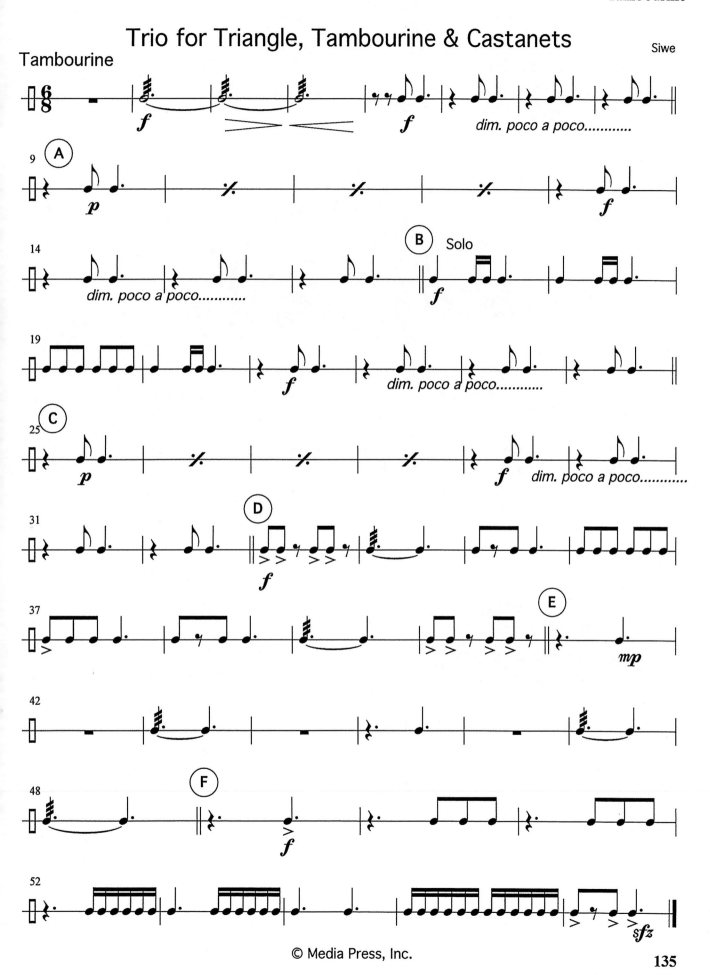

135

Castanets

History

Castanets are made from hard, resonant wood, e.g., chestnut, and are often associated with Spain and other Hispanic countries. Similar instruments were used in ancient Roman times, but they may have been made of metal as well as wood. A pair of castanet 'chips' are pitched slightly apart with two holes drilled through each extended tab. Cord passing through these holes can be looped around a players thumb and manipulated with the fingers to produce a rhythmic accompaniment. For practical reasons, modern percussionists use 'chips' mounted on wooden handles which they strike against their knee or body. It is also possible to mount the castanets on a wooden frame (machine castanets) enabling the player to strike them with his/her fingers or with soft marimba mallets.

Types and sizes

Castanets are bought or made in pairs. The chips run in sizes from 2.5 inches to 3 inches in diameter. The smaller the chip, the higher the sound. Mountings can vary. Two chips mounted at the end of small wooden handles provide the player with an instrument on which clear, rhythmic passages are easy to execute. This is the type of castanet that most professionals recommend. The type of castanet in which the handle extends so that the chips strike it rather than each other, i.e., paddle castanets, makes rolling easy, but rhythmic passages and single notes are more difficult to perform cleanly. 'Castanet machines' mount the chips so that they strike each other to create the sound. Because of the mounting, the sound from machine castanets is less resonant and sustained rolls are more difficult.

Castanet Machine

Grip

Castanets are held one in each hand near the middle of the handle so that, if necessary, the first finger can touch the base of the tab. The knuckles face upward. If there is a difference in pitch between the two castanets, the higher-pitched instrument is placed in the dominant hand.

Performance techniques

To perform slow moving rhythmic passages that do not require any embellishments, use just one castanet. Hold the castanet in one hand and strike the chip with the tips of the three middle fingers. If using a 'paddle castanet,' hold it parallel to the floor and strike the paddle just behind the chip with the tips of the three middle fingers using a sharp, downward stroke.

For fast moving rhythmic passages use two castanets. Players often use a chair rung or some support for the foot so that the castanets can be easily struck on the thigh. The stroke is a short wrist movement. To achieve the cleanest sound, a player may 'dead stroke. into the thigh so that the castanet does not rebound thus producing sharper, cleaner sounds. Single-line, rhythmic passages are played using the same right/left hand approach as for the snare drum.

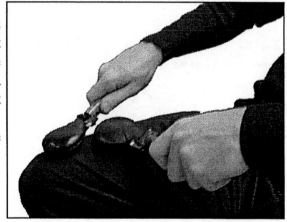

Rolls are played hand-to-hand. Placing the first finger lightly on the end of the tab will produce a fuller sounding roll. To roll with paddle castanets, the player suspends them with the chips hanging down and moves the handles rapidly back and forth. To cleanly end the roll, the paddles are brought against the body. On machine castanets, short rolls are possible by 'strumming' the fingers of one or both hands. If the castanets are used to evoke the image of the Spanish dancer, players often add grace notes and other embellishments to the written music.

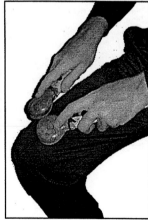

Castanet Exercises

Siwe

Etude for Castanets I

Exercises for Castanets

(Castanet Exercises, p. 2)

Roll Exercise

Etude for Castanets II

Trio for Triangle, Tambourine & Castanets

Siwe

Claves

History

Claves are "idiophones of Cuban origin consisting of two cylindrical hardwood sticks" (The New Grove, 2nd. Ed.) The cylinders range in size from 6 to 10 inches with a diameter of 1 to 1.5 inches and are made from hard woods such as grenadilla and rosewood, with the latter the professional instrument of choice. Though classified as non-pitched, their resonant, high frequency sound has a definite pitch with each cylinder being slightly different. Used in Afro-Cuban music, the claves play a role similar to the African bell as the all-important time keeper. In Cuba, the 'son clave' and its reverse the 'rumba clave' are important dance rhythms establishing the beat and giving direction to

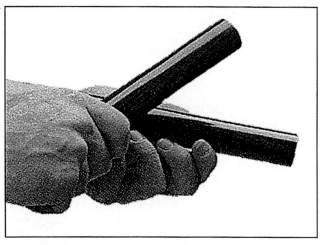

the rhythmic flow. A rhythmic variation, the Brazilian 'Bossa Nova', is often played on the snare drum in imitation of the clave sound. Composers use the claves to evoke sounds of Latin America (e.g. Revueltas' *Sensemayá*, 1937) or as a unique timbre (e.g. Varèse's *Ionisation*, 1931).

Performance Techniques

Face the palm of one hand upward and curl the fingers and thumb to create a small resonating chamber. Lay one of the claves lightly across this pocket, centering it for balance and stability. Grasp the other clave as you would a violin bow at a point just off center. Use this clave to strike the resting clave at mid-point. The stroke is primarily a wrist action with a quick rebound to insure maximum resonance.

Ratchet
(cog rattle)

History

The ratchet, or cog rattle, is classified by musicologists as a scraped idiophone. In Europe, "ratchets serve in the Orthodox Church; in Roman churches they replace the bells during Holy Week." (The New Grove, 2nd Ed.) " The percussionist of the salon orchestra had long ago included the small ratchet in his set of sound effects (Joseph Strauss: *Plappermäulchen Polka*)" (Peinkofer and Tannigel,152). Richard Strauss made good use of the ratchet in his 1894 tone poem, *Till Eulenspiegel*.

Performance Techniques

There are two types of ratchet. One has a handle attached that allows the instrument to be twirled with one hand, using a small rotary wrist motion. This type of ratchet comes in a range of sizes, from small to large. The larger the ratchet, the louder and deeper the sound. The other ratchet type has a small crank handle attached that one turns as if winding up a fishing reel. There are large and small versions available in this style, but the sound is inferior to the twirled version. The advantage of the crank style is greater control of the sound duration. In addition, it comes with a clamp that allows it to be attached to the rim of a bass drum or trap table edge. Ratchets are mostly constructed from soft woods, but metal versions are also available.

Slapstick
(whip)

History
"The sound of a whip has been connected with musical activities for many centuries" (New Groves, 2nd Ed.). Also known as a slapstick, it was a standard sound effect device in the days of vaudeville and circus bands. Composers used the slapstick to imitate a whip crack (Leroy Anderson: *Sleigh Ride*, 1950) or for its own special sound (Varèse: *Ionisation*. 1931).

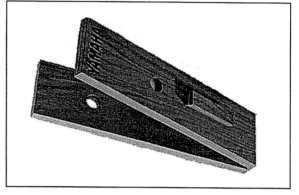

Performance Techniques
Slapsticks range in size from ca. 14 inches to ca. 20 inches in length and from 2 inches to 6 inches in diameter. Made from two slats of thin, hardwood hinged at one end, they are either made with or without a spring mechanism. The larger instruments preferred by professionals have grooves cut lengthwise on the inside of the two slats to help disperse the trapped pockets of air, plus two handles centered on the outside. The spring type has a handle extending below the hinge. The spring type is playable with one hand, but has a weaker sound and offers the player less control.

For the spring type, grasp the handle of the slapstick with the movable slat facing upward, toward the player. To activate, make a quick, downward arm and hand motion similar to that used to crack a whip. For the professional slapstick, hold the instrument by the handles at face level with the slats about 8 inches apart at the widest. Bring the two slats together with a quick motion. The amount of force (along with the size of the instrument) will determine the level of intensity.

Slit Drum
(African log/wood drum)

History
Though its name includes the word 'drum', 'Slit Drums' are idiophones (not membranophones) that were originally hollowed from whole tree trunks. In Africa, the two sides of the opening (or slit) "are carved to different thicknesses so that at least two pitches can be produced"
(New Grove, 2nd Ed.). Varieties of slit-drums are found in Africa, Asia, Polynesia and the Americas (e.g., Aztec teponaztli). They are used for both musical and ritual purposes and, in Africa and South America, as a signaling device. Today's slit-drums are often created by constructing a long, rectangular wooden box with a top piece cut to form two or more 'tongues'.

Performance Techniques
Most slit drums used in orchestras and bands are the constructed, box type that have only one or two 'tongues', i.e. one or two pitches. Specialty percussion catalogs offer drums in various sizes and arrays with precise pitch possibilities. It is important to determine from your score whether the part is notated for a precise pitch or the drum is used only for its unique timbre.

To insure the best, most resonant sound from a slit drum, place the instrument on a padded surface, with the top of the drum about waist high for ease of playing. Strike the instrument with a yarn mallet of medium hardness. Soft or hard yarn mallets, as well as soft rubber mallets, will produce slight variations of dynamics and timbre. Avoid using any mallet or stick that would damage the soft, wooden tongues. Find the most resonant playing spot for each tongue and strike it with a rebounding stroke that insures a full, consistent sound.

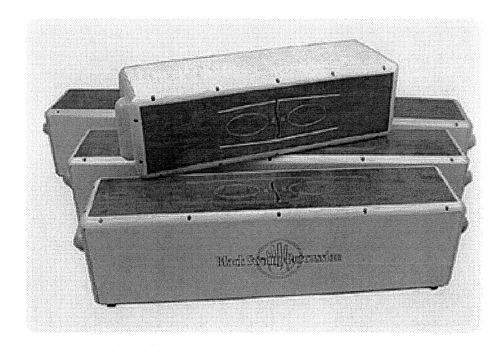

Temple Blocks

History

"Temple blocks are usually made of camphor wood and brightly painted." (New Grove, 2nd Ed.) This soft wood is easily damaged and plastic substitutes are now used for school level instruments. Temple blocks are used in both Taoist and Buddhist rites. In Chinese they are called 'Mu yü' (wooden fish), in Korean mo ko (earlier versions resembled wooden fish). The Japanese 'Mo kugyo' is similar, but made from harder woods and as a result have a higher, sharper sound. During the early 20th century, temple blocks were found in sets, usually five, and played by drum set artists in jazz combos, orchestras and dance bands. In orchestra and band music they played both musical (Berg: *Lulu*, 1928) and sound effect (Grofé: *Grand Canyon Suite*. 1931) roles.

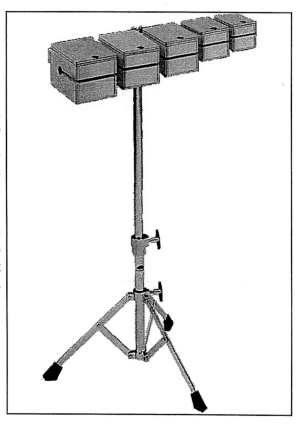

Performance Techniques

Temple blocks commonly used in orchestra and bands come in graduated sets of four to five blocks that range in size from three inches in diameter to around seven or eight inches. Usually mounted on a metal rack attached to a height adjustable floor stand, the blocks need careful handling. The stands are easily knocked over and the blocks, plastic or wood, can be damaged as a result. The tops of the blocks should be around waist-high for ease of playing. It is possible to remove individual blocks from their racks and set them on a padded surface such as a trap table. Place the wing-nuts and insulating washers in a small zip-lock bag to keep them from getting lost. You will need them to remount the blocks.

The blocks are normally struck with medium-hard, rubber marimba mallets. Other sticks or mallets e,g, hard yarn marimba mallets, give slight timbre and attack sound variations. The player must, as with timpani, 'work out' their sticking so that they can move from block to block with ease. The mallet heads should strike the top center of each block with a motion that allows the mallet head to rebound, creating the most resonant sound possible.

Wood Block

History

Hardwood, rectangular idiophones, "wood blocks are related to the rectangular wooden slit-drums that are used as time-beaters by the Han Chinese (ban), hence the occasional specification of 'Chinese wood blocks'." (The New Grove, 2nd. Ed.) Classified as non-pitched, wood blocks are used in both serious and popular music. Early jazz drummers played solo 'licks' on wood blocks (or wooden tubes) during the rag-time era of the 20th century. Even today, show drummers play wood blocks with drum sticks to 'back' tap dance acts. Sometimes designated in scores by the Italian term 'legno', wood blocks are orchestrated for their bright sound, high pitch, color and clear articulation. Today, pitched chromatic sets of wood blocks are sold through percussion specialty catalogs.

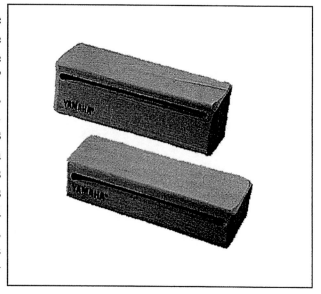

Performance Techniques

Wood blocks range in size from the piccolo wood blocks (ca. 4 inches) to large, custom blocks (ca. 12 inches). A well equipped percussion section should have at least two blocks of different sizes.

If possible, hold the wood block in the palm of one hand and play it with a hard, rubber mallet. Other beaters, such as hard-yarn vibraphone mallets, or snare drum sticks offer subtle timbre variances. Strike the block just off center near the open edge. Exploring the instrument's striking surface provides the player with a variety of possible sounds. If the musical passage is too difficult to be played with one hand, place the block on a padded surface and use two identical beaters, striking the block as close to the same 'beating spot' as possible to obtain a consistent sound.

Claves

Etude for Small Wooden Instruments

Siwe

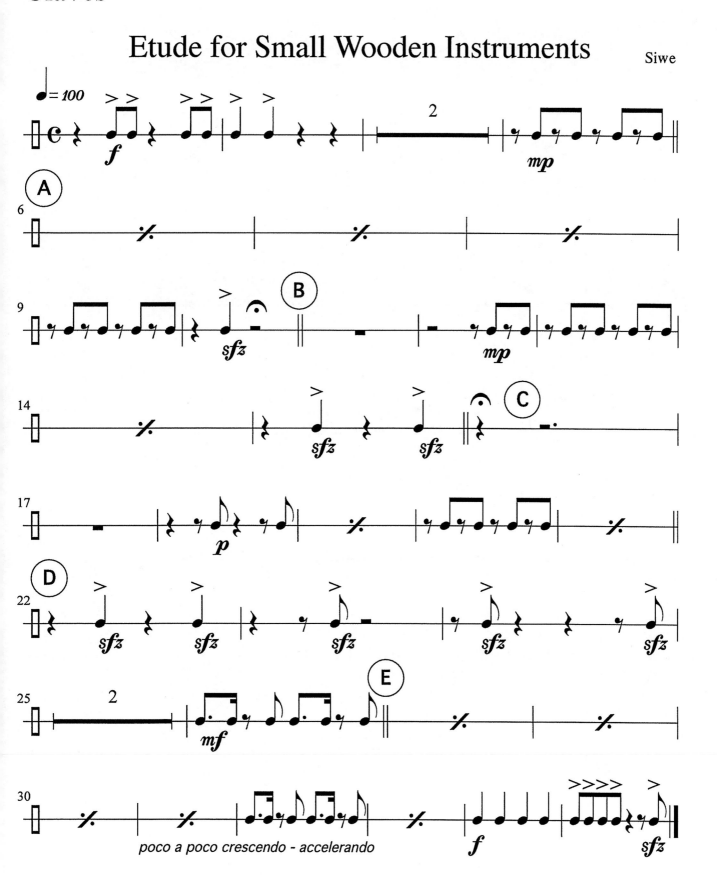

Ratchet

Etude for Small Wooden Instruments

ff *poco a poco crescendo - accelerando*

Slapstick

poco a poco crescendo - accelerando

Slit Drum
(African log/wood drum)

Siwe

Etude for Small Wooden Instruments

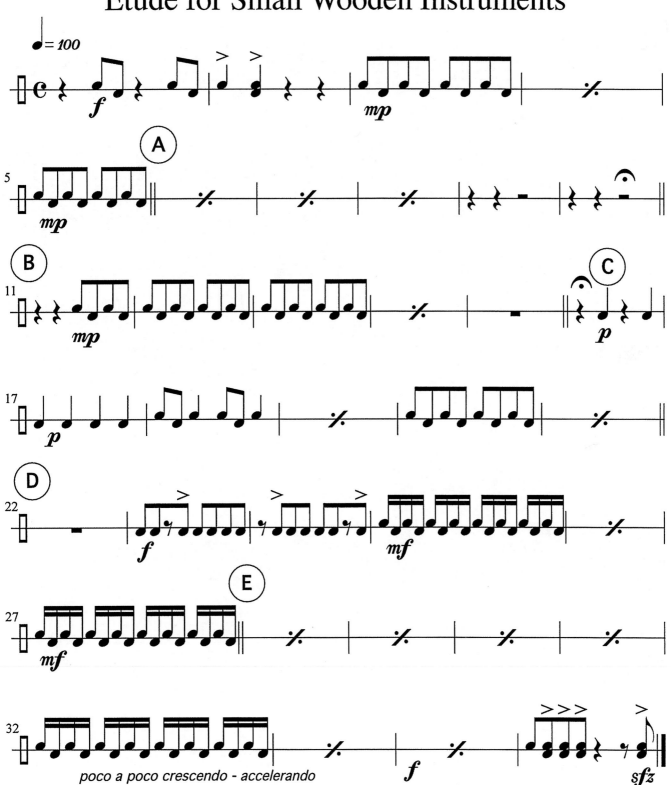

poco a poco crescendo - accelerando

Temple Blocks

Etude for Small Wooden Instruments

Siwe

poco a poco crescendo - accelerando

Wood Blocks

Etude for Small Wooden Instruments

Siwe

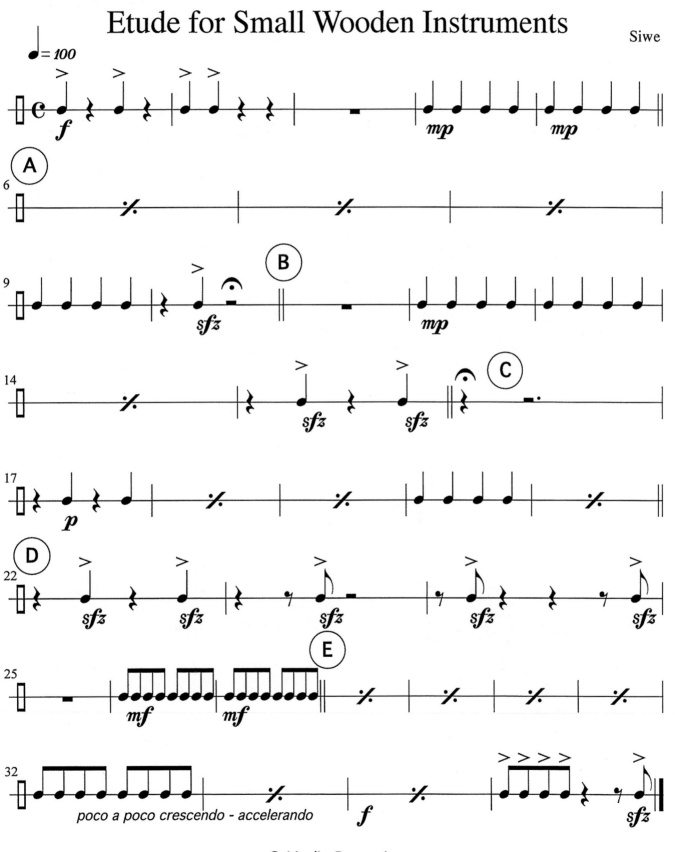

Anvil
(metal block)

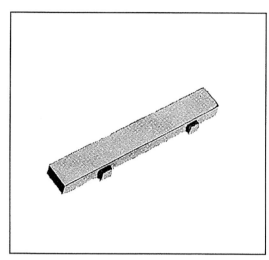

History

A metallic hammering from the blacksmith's forge was once a familiar sound in villages and small towns throughout Asia and the Western world. Composers, like Wagner, used the anvil to evoke this clangorous din. "In the *Transformation Scene* of *Das Rheingold* one hears the tremendous crescendo of the anvil chorus of the *Nibelungs* offstage: a group of eighteen players beating eighteen anvils..." (Peinkofer and Tannigel 1976, 136). Auber calls for the anvil in his opera *Le Maçon* and Varèse in his wind ensemble work *Hyperprism* (1923). Difficulty in locating and moving these substantial pieces of iron has led professional percussionists to substitute iron bars, pipes or even railroad track sections for the anvil.

Performance Techniques

For safety, center the metal instrument on a sturdy, padded trap table. Pieces of foam rubber material placed at the nodal points will help to insure a full, resonant sound. With brass mallets, locate the best playing area and strike it, using a sharp, wrist action to create a rebounding stroke.

Cowbell
(cencerros, metal blocks)

History

"Ever since man has herded domestic animals, bells have been hung on them to identify their location by sound or to protect them from evil spirits." (Peinkofer and Tannigel 1976, 130). Cowbells (or herd bells) are made from a variety of materials, both woods and metals. Used throughout the world, they have many names, almglocken, cencerro, herdenglocken, kuhschelle, sonnaille, etc., and are constructed in a variety of shapes: conical, cylindrical, spherical and trapezoidal. Used descriptively by nineteenth century composers (sometimes to evoke bucolic scenes), cowbells are used today for their own unique timbres. A popular version most often used in dance and Latin bands is the cencerro. An angular, trapezoid shape, it is made to be struck with a stick and has a dry, sharp sound, far removed from the more resonant herd bells.

Performance Techniques

For the best sound and control, hold the cowbell in one hand with the opening upward, pointing slightly toward the audience. With the butt end of a drumstick, strike the bell in the middle or toward the open end. A variety of sounds are possible by changing the beating spot and varying the hand pressure. To dampen its resonance, a cloth may be inserted into the 'bell' end. Arrays of cowbells may be assembled and mounted on frames or just placed on a padded trap table. Strips of Velcro can help stabilize the bells, avoiding unwanted movement.

Crotales
(cymbales antiques)

Crotales

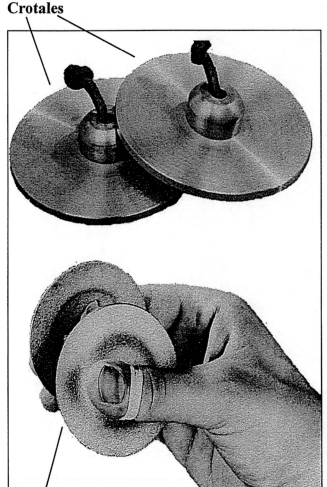

Finger cymbals

History

Cast bronze disks, tuned to specific pitches, what we call 'crotales, ' are thought to have been used as accompaniment to the dance. Their history is an ancient one, with extant disks dating from ca. 850 B.C. Often played in pairs, crotales can also be found today in sets of up to two octaves. "The written range is c1 to c3, and they sound two octaves higher" (Beck 1995, 29). Finger cymbals are similar to crotales but are thinner and smaller in size. They are sold in pairs tuned to approximately the same pitch so that when struck together the dissonant 'beating' effect creates a 'shimmering' sound.

Performance Techniques

To play just one crotale, suspend it using a strip of knotted cowhide, or similar cord. Grip the cord with the thumb and first finger near the dome and turn the flat side toward you. With a brass mallet (or hard rubber mallet) strike the flat surface near one edge. As the crotale sounds, it is possible to create a vibrato by slowly shaking the disk. If using two crotales, hold one as described above. With the edge of the other disk, strike the flat Finger Cymbals surface of the first and allow both disks to vibrate freely.

Crotales can be mounted on a simple post and frame apparatus. Be sure that the posts are insulated and that the disks are not too tightly secured. Strike the array of disks using brass mallets. Use a light, rebounding stroke.

Gong

History

"The name 'gong' had its origin in Java (Blades 1970, 93). This ancient, cast-bronze instrument is noted in China early in the sixth century. Classified as singly-struck, pitched idiophones, gongs are found not only in gamelans and Western orchestras but also in homes and museums. Many gongs have raised centers. Some are flat-faced; all are circular, with angled or straight flanges. The thickness of the metal requires a beater (or mallet) of substantial mass. Repertoire that calls for tuned gongs includes: Puccini's *Madama Butterfly* (1904) and *Turandot* (1924), Saint-Saëns' *La princesse jaune* (1872), R. Strauss's *Die Frau ohne Schatten* (1914). In some scores the term gong designates a non-pitched, small tam tam, e.g. Varèse's *Ionisation* (1929-31). Inconsistent use of terms (whether gongs or tam tams) has caused some confusion. A careful examination of the score may be necessary to determine the composer's intent.

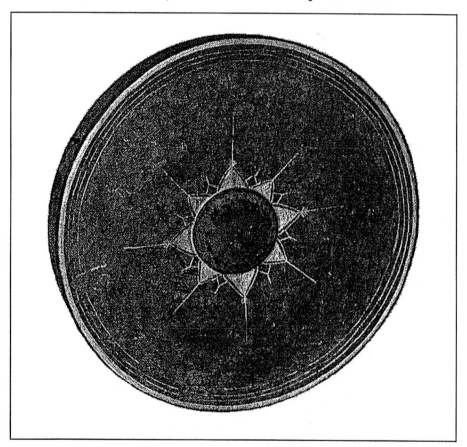

Performance Techniques

Suspend the gong from a sturdy, height-adjustable stand using parachute cord, or similar strong, insulated rope. Select a gong beater whose size and weight are apropos to the size and mass of the gong. With a motion similar to that used on the bass drum, strike the gong directly in its center, allowing the stick to rebound freely. To dampen the sound use both hands to grasp the edge and center of the gong.

Suspended Cymbal
(see Cymbals)

Tam tam

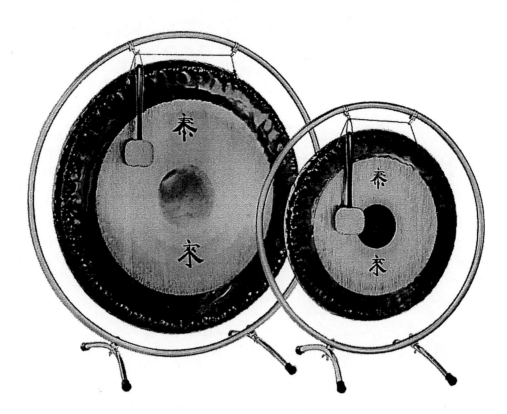

History

"The tam tam differs from the pitched, dome gong (or simply gong) by having no dome-like indentation in the center and thus having no definable pitch" (Peinkofer and Tannigel 1976,126). Bronze disks, sized from ca. eight inches to ca. 80 inches, tam tams are somewhat thinner than gongs, having a slightly curved surface and a small, angled flange. " The gong appeared in orchestra scores towards the close of the eighteenth century in Gossac's *Funeral Music for Mirabeau* (1791) and Steibelt's *Romeo and Juliet* (1793) (Blades 1970, 383). In the twentieth century, composers began to use the tam tam in unusual ways, e.g. tremolo (Holst's *The Planets*, 1914), with wood sticks (Stravinsky's *Petrouchka*, 1911) rub with cardboard tube (Burge's *Sources III*, 1967), dip into water (Harrison's *Labyrinth No. 3*, 1941). Pieces have even been written for solo tam tam, e.g. Stockhausen's *Mikrophonie I*, 1964) and O'Donnell's *Microtimbre I*, 1972).

Performance Techniques

Most bands and orchestras own at least one tam tam, usually medium to large in size. Large tam tams are expensive, easily broken and thus need special care. A sturdy, adjustable metal frame on wheels is recommended. Beaters (or mallets) used by school percussionists should be covered with felt or yarn and have a soft, rubber core. To play the tam tam, stand on one side of it with your free hand directly behind the disk's midpoint. Usually the best place to strike the tam tam is on its face side, just off center. Silently place the mallet head on the striking spot. Using the arm, pull the mallet head back from the instrument. To activate, allow the mallet head to fall naturally, striking the selected spot. The distance the mallet head travels will determine the volume. Do not use excessive force. Tam tams, like cymbals, have a maximum dynamic level. Attempts to increase the sound using excessive force will only damage the instrument. To dampen the sound, grasp the center of the tam tam with both hands.

Anvil

Etude for Metal Instruments

Siwe

Cowbell

Etude for Metal Instruments

Siwe

Crotales

Etude for Metal Instruments

Siwe

fine

Gong

Etude for Metal Instruments

Siwe

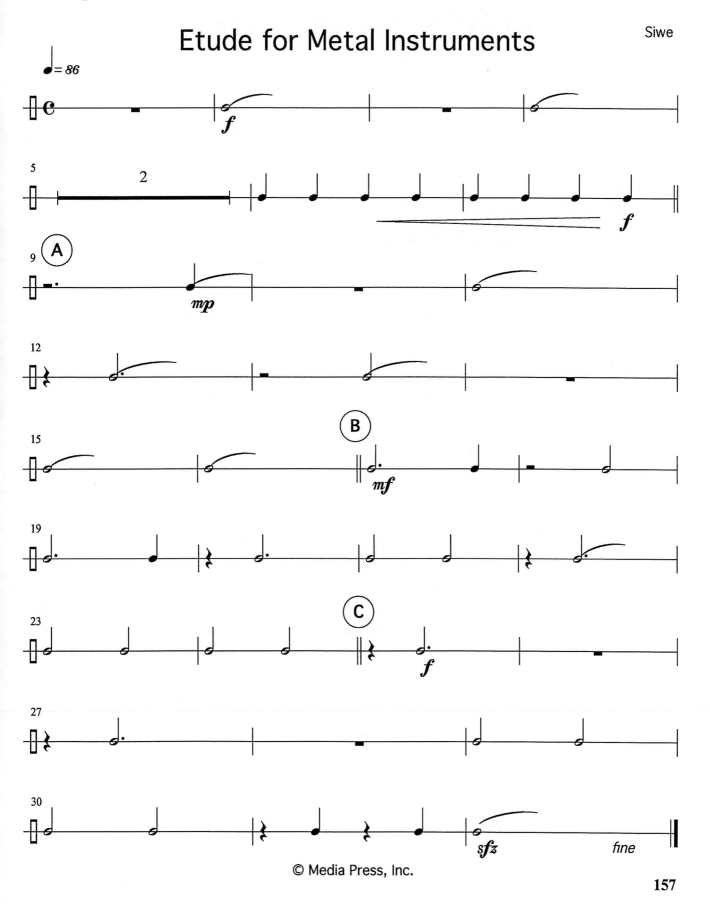

Susp. Cym.

Etude for Metal Instruments

Siwe

Tam Tam

Etude for Metal Instruments

Siwe

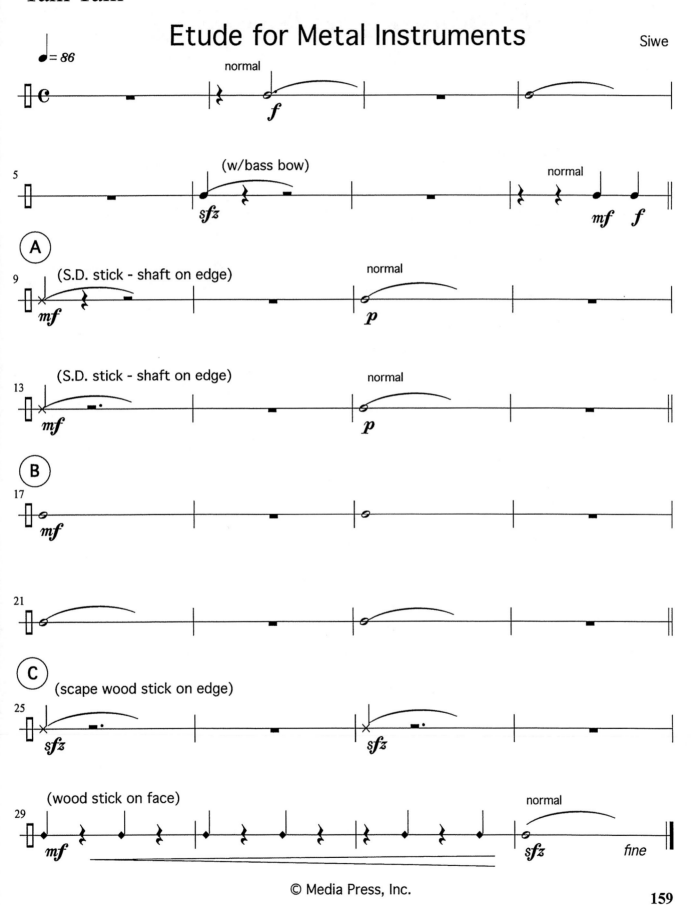

Mallet-Keyboard Range Chart

Orchestra Bells
(sounds 15 va)

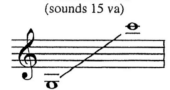

Tubular Chimes
(sounds 8 va)

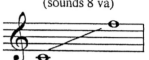

Xylophone
(sounds 8 va)

Vibraphone

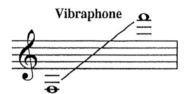

Marimba

Marimba

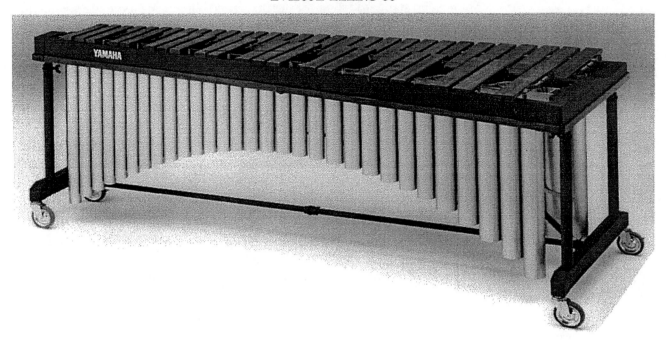

History

By definition, a marimba is a type of xylophone. It is believed to have originated in Africa where it was noted as early as the 13th century. It most likely arrived in the Americas with the slave trade, making the greatest impact in Southern Mexico and Central America. The instruments first documented in the Americas resembled those from Africa, i.e. rows of bars assembled into scales, suspended on simple wooden frames, with gourd (or wood) resonators under each note. Common to both the African and American versions is the mirliton device located in the resonator causing the note to 'buzz' when struck. When marimba bars were arranged to form a chromatic scale and by whom cannot be firmly fixed, however its invention allowed western style music to be performed. Early on, marimbas played an important part in the music of southern Mexico and the Central American countries south to Costa Rica; "it is a commonly recognized fact that the marimba is an essential element of the musical life of Guatemala and has been since the mid-nineteenth century". (Kastner 1989, 9). In 1908, a Guatemalan marimba band, The Hurtado Brothers, toured North America. Their concerts, and later recordings on the Victor label, helped to popularize the marimba in the United States. An important figure in the development of the marimba in the U.S. was Claire Omar Musser (1901-1998). The Percussive Arts Society dubbed him "the single most influential marimbist, marimba composer, and marimba designer in the history of the instrument". Musser designed marimbas for the Chicago-based J. C. Deagan Company; taught at Northwestern University; and assembled, trained and conducted large marimba orchestras (up to 100 players and instruments), concertizing both in the U.S. and in Europe. He wrote and arranged marimba music, presented solo recitals and spent most of his life promoting the marimba. In 1940, Paul Creston composed a *Concertino* for solo marimba and orchestra. A small number of concertos followed, but it wasn't until the 1960s when the marimba began to again attract the attention of serious composers. This was due, in part, to Keiko Abe, a Japanese marimba virtuoso, who, in 1962, commissioned solo marimba works from a number of well-known composers and brought a new level of artistry to the instrument. The last forty years of the twentieth century saw the solo marimba repertoire expand at an amazing rate. Championed by numerous virtuosi, the marimba continues to gain an ever-widening audience.

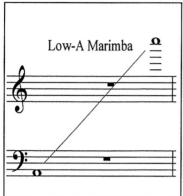

Low-A Marimba

Range/Sound

There is no standard range for the marimba. Numerous models exist having chromatic ranges that vary from one to six-plus octaves. Except for the bass marimba, most versions include the area around middle c, with a popular student model encompassing low A to c4, a range of 4 1/3 octaves. The marimba sound has been described as 'mellow', or 'organ like in tone.' Perhaps this is due to its comparison with its more 'clangorous' cousin, the xylophone. It is tuned differently than the xylophone, with an emphasis on the fundamental and the octave overtone. All marimbas have individual resonators beneath each note making it much easier to sustain a sound. Because of its blending tone quality, the marimba is not often used as a solo voice within band and orchestra literature, but is orchestrated in a supporting role instead. It does serve well as a truly solo instrument when placed in front of the ensemble. Above all, the marimba is the best training instrument for mallet-keyboard techniques. It has a vast literature, both pedagogical and artistic, dwarfing that for the xylophone and other mallet-keyboard instruments combined. Its technical demands are greater as are its musical possibilities. It is recommended that students begin their mallet-keyboard training on the marimba.

Mallets

Marimba bars are made from rosewood, as are xylophone bars, but the wood selected is less dense and the bars, especially the lower octaves, thinner. Mallets used on marimbas are normally covered with yarn or made with rubber heads. Hard mallets, such as those used on the xylophone, damage the bars. Mallet shafts are made from rattan (preferred), birch, or plastic. They vary little in length (10" to 17").

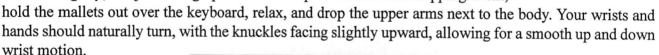

Grip

To grip the marimba mallet, grasp the shaft near the end using the thumb and index finger. Wrap the other fingers lightly around the shaft without allowing much, if any, of it to protrude. Both right and left hand grips are the same. Do not grip the shaft too tightly; use just enough pressure to keep the mallet from slipping. Next, hold the mallets out over the keyboard, relax, and drop the upper arms next to the body. Your wrists and hands should naturally turn, with the knuckles facing slightly upward, allowing for a smooth up and down wrist motion.

Three and Four Mallet Grips

Beginning marimba music is almost exclusively written for two mallets, but some three and four mallet parts occasionally occur in school-level literature. There are a number of excellent grips used to play four mallet parts.

If the student studies with a private marimba teacher, they should be allowed to continue to play four mallets as endorsed by their teacher. If not, the simple cross grip is easiest to teach and to learn, and will facilitate the performance of any simple three or four-mallet parts that might appear in the literature. The cross grip is as follows: For the right hand, place two mallets parallel to each other on the marimba natural keys allowing the shafts to extend out as much as possible. Lift the shaft end of the left hand (inside) mallet and cross it over the right one at about a third of the distance from the end. Grasp the mallets at the point that they cross, with the index finger between the two mallets, the thumb opposite the index finger and the other fingers wrapped around both shafts. The grip for the left hand is a mirror of the right hand. You will notice that the inside mallets for both hands feel the most secure since the thumb and index finger form a fulcrum as with the snare drum grip. To spread the mallet heads farther apart, the player rolls the thumb over the shaft so that

both thumb and index finger lie between the two shafts. The arm position for three and four mallets is the same as for two-mallet playing, but the knuckles now face directly upward. The stroke action is still a smooth up-and-down wrist motion.

Playing Area/Tone Production/Stance

For the best tone quality, the marimba bars are struck in the center, or for the lower octaves, just off center. Fast passages sometimes demand that players strike the very edges of the accidental bars, however, the tone quality suffers and professionals avoid using the edges when possible. The stroke used is an up-and-down wrist action. There is very little natural rebound off the bars. The player must lift the mallet head quickly away from the bar to insure a resonant tone. The length of the marimba keyboard requires players to move with agility, up and down the keyboard. This is accomplished by shuffling side to side so that the player is centered in front of the bars being played. It is important that the player stand erect and avoid bending over the bars. Also, avoid crowding the keyboard in the upper register, i. e., standing too close forcing the elbows to protrude behind the back. As the player moves from the low end of the marimba to the high register, the space between their body and the keyboard should increase. The elbows remain positioned next to the body and the distance the mallet heads move from naturals to accidentals remains constant.

Sticking

Players must be taught to alternate right and left hands as much as possible, even though beginning parts are sometimes playable with just one mallet. Practicing scales and arpeggios is helpful in learning how to cross over and under to reach adjacent notes. When solving sticking problems, avoid playing two or more notes with one hand. Alternate sticking is best and will insure smooth-sounding scale passages at fast tempi. Passages can begin with either right or left hands; whatever works best is the rule.

Notation

It is common to notate marimba music similarly to that for piano, leaving it up to the player to decide which notes to sustain by 'rolling' and which to leave resonate naturally. All two mallet 'rolls' are played hand to hand, similar to that for timpani. When rolling double stops or chords, be sure that the top note sounds first.

Marimba - top

Mallet Exercises I

Siwe

Scales and Arpeggios

Marimba - bottom

Mallet Exercises I

Scales and arpeggios

Siwe

Mallet Exercises II
Double Stops, Rolls

Marimba - top

Siwe

Mallet Chops

Marimba - top

Siwe

poco a poco accelerando al fine

Fine

Mallet Chops

Marimba - bottom

Siwe

poco a poco accelerando al fine

Blue Funk

Marimba

Siwe

Marimba

Latin Island

Siwe

Marimba

Minor Swing

Siwe

Marimba

Siwe's Shuffle

Siwe

Marimba

Straight Rock

Siwe

Xylophone

History

Named for the Greek words 'xylon', (wood) and 'phone' (a sound), the xylophone is an idiophone consisting of a series of tuned wooden bars arranged to form a musical scale. It is normally struck with two or more mallets (hammers).

The origin of the xylophone is disputed, being either Asian or African. Found on both continents, as well as Central and South America, its native versions take many forms. Some xylophones are simply a few bars of wood laid over an open pit or on a bed of straw; others have wooden bars with gourd resonators attached and suspended in a frame. Xylophones similar to those used in today's orchestras and bands began to be noticed in the West as early as the sixteenth century. "The first known visual representation of a xylophone in Europe is a woodcut by Hans Holbein the Younger entitled, "Dance of Death", dating from about 1523". (Beck 1995, 352). The instrument was popularized by "a Russian Jew named Gusikow, whose performances drew favorable comment from Chopin and Liszt..." (Blades 1970, 307). An early example of xylophone writing can be found in the 1805 cantata *Der Einsiedler* (The Hermit) by the German composer, Ferdinand Kauer (1751-1831). Later Saint-Saëns employed the instrument in his famous *Danse Macabre* (1874) and again used it to depict fossil bones in *The Carnival of the Animals* (1886). As with other percussion instruments, twentieth century composers wrote extensively for the xylophone in both orchestra and chamber music, utilizing it not only for its unique timbre, but as another tonal voice, e.g., Stravinsky's *Petrouchka* (1911), Gershwin's *Porgy and Bess* (1935), Bartok's *Sonata* (1937), Copland's *Appalachian Spring* (1945). In the early days of recorded music, the xylophone became a popular solo instrument, especially in the United States. Military and concert bands employed xylophone soloists such as the famous virtuoso, George Hamilton Green. Early concert xylophones were made with bars cut from the finest rosewood trees, suspended over metal resonators in a configuration similar to the piano keyboard. The J. C. Deagan Company of Chicago, Illinois was an industry leader in producing quality instruments for the American market.

Range/Sound

The model of xylophone most often found in today's bands and orchestras has a chromatic range of three and one-half octaves from f1 to c5 (notated f to c4). Xylophones with ranges of 2.5 to 5 octaves are made as well, with a 4-octave instrument being the one preferred by professionals. All are written as transposing instruments, i.e. they sound an octave higher than notated. Also, all have a bright, piercing sound when played with the standard hard-rubber mallet. This is due in part to their tuning, which for American instruments emphasizes the 12th partial in addition to the fundamental. It is not unusual to find a xylophone part that has notes written outside the range of the available instrument. Playing these an octave lower, or higher is acceptable, as long as the shape of the phrase is given consideration.

Mallets

To produce the idiomatic sound of the Western xylophone, the player should use mallets with hard rubber or synthetic heads. The shafts can be of rattan or plastic. Other mallet types such as hard yarn or cord wound mallets are useful in certain musical settings that demand a change in tone color. They should not be used to create softer dynamics, but rather, the player should learn to control the intensity levels required with the normal hard mallet.

Grip

The grip used for xylophone mallets is very similar to that used for holding snare drum sticks. Grasp the mallet shaft about one third the distance from the end using the thumb and index finger. Wrap the other fingers lightly around the shaft. Both hands are the same. Do not grip the shaft too tightly; use just enough pressure to keep the mallet from slipping. Next, hold the mallets out over the keyboard, relax and drop the upper arms next to the body. Your wrists and hands should naturally turn, with the knuckles facing slightly upward, allowing for a smooth up and down wrist motion.

Three- and Four-Mallet Grips

Most xylophone parts are written for two mallets, though some three- and four-mallet parts can be found in school-level literature. The simple cross grip is the easiest for beginning players. See **Marimba** for details.

Playing Area/Tone Production

For the best tone quality, strike directly in the center of the bars. The hard mallets and thick bars allow players to strike the sharp keys near the ends of the bars without a serious adverse effect on tone quality. This can be useful in fast-moving-passages. The striking motion used is a simple up-and-down wrist motion. There is some natural rebound from the impact of the mallet head, but not very much. The player must lift the mallet head quickly back from the bar to insure a resonant tone.

Sticking

Players must be taught to alternate right and left hands as much as possible, even though beginning parts are sometimes playable with just one mallet. Practicing scales and arpeggios is helpful in learning how to cross over and under to reach adjacent notes. When working out sticking problems, avoid playing two or more notes with one hand. Alternate sticking is best and will insure smooth sounding scale passages at fast tempi. Passages can begin with either right or left hands; whatever works best is the rule.

Notation

For sustained notes, composers use both the "three slashes" and "tr", the sign for tremolo. These are performed as single-stroke rolls similar to timpani strokes. Many times half notes and whole notes are notated, but rarely are these interpreted as rolls. The xylophone is a transposing instrument, sounding one octave higher than written.

Xylophone

Mallet Exercises I
Scales and Arpeggios

Siwe

Xylophone

Mallet Exercises II
Double Stops, Rolls

Siwe

Fine

D.C. al Fine

Xylophone

Mallet Chops

Siwe

poco a poco accelerando al fine

Fine

Xylophone

Blue Funk

Siwe

Xylophone

Latin Island

Siwe

Xylophone

Minor Swing

Siwe

(hard yarns) (swing dotted rhythms)

Xylophone

Siwe's Shuffle

Siwe

Xylophone

Straight Rock

Siwe

Orchestra Bells
(glockenspiel)

History

Orchestra Bells (Ger. - *glockenspiel*) are metallophones "...consisting of a series of tuned steel bars arranged in two rows, as are the keys of a piano..." (Marcuse 1964, 210). Its Western ancestor, at least in sound, are the small bells of medieval Europe that evolved into the church carillon; but a more recent origin would be the bell lyra, "...which was introduced into the bands of the German infantry sometime after 1870..." (Peinkofer and Tannigel 1976, 53). This marching set of bells (later metal bars) was strung on frames and played with a small, hard mallet. Mozart scored for a keyboard version of the glockenspiel in his opera *The Magic Flute* (1791), the bells representing Papageno's magic chimes. With this instrument, metal bars were struck from below with hard hammers using a piano-like mechanism. These two forms of orchestra bells existed side by side from the middle of the 18th century. The keyboard version slowly disappeared from use and is "...little used today, the tone of the mallet-played instrument being superior". (Blades 1970, 398).

Range

The range of the orchestra bells manufactured in the U.S. is two and one-half octaves notated from g to c3, sounding two octaves higher. There are a few European models that add a perfect fourth to the upper range, with some models having a pedal-dampening mechanism similar to the vibraphone's. Since the history of the orchestra bells includes a keyboard instrument with a greater range than today's mallet-played version, there are passages from the late 18th and 19th century opera and orchestra literature that need to be reworked. Often the player will find that the passage extends beyond the range of the instrument. As with the xylophone, playing these passages an octave lower or higher is acceptable, as long as the shape of the phrase is given consideration.

Mallets

The standard mallets for play on the orchestra bells are made of brass with rattan, birch or plastic handles. Other mallets such as hard plastic, are sometimes used if the passage is exposed or if a softer, celesta-like sound is desired.

Grip

The grip used for orchestra bell mallets is very similar to that used for holding snare drum sticks. Grasp the mallet shaft about one third the distance from the end using the thumb and index finger. Wrap the other fingers lightly around the shaft. Both hands are the same. Do not grip the shaft too tightly; use just enough pressure to keep the mallet from slipping. Next, hold the mallets out over the keyboard, relax, and drop the upper arms next to the body. Your wrists and hands should naturally turn, with the knuckles facing slightly upward, allowing for a smooth up and down wrist motion.

Three- and Four-Mallet Grips

There are few three-note chords written for bells and, even rarer, four-note chords. If necessary, use the simple cross grip, which is the easiest for beginning players. See **Marimba** for details.

Playing Area/Tone Production/Stance

Orchestra bell bars are always struck in the center. The stroke used is an up-and-down wrist action. There is very little natural rebound off the bars; the player must lift the mallet head quickly away from the bar to insure a resonant tone and to avoid creating ambient noise caused by the suspension system. It is important that the player stand erect and avoid bending over the bars.

Sticking

Beginning players must be taught to alternate right and left hands as much as possible, even though simple parts are sometimes playable with just one mallet. Practicing scales and arpeggios is helpful in learning how to cross over and under to reach adjacent notes. Passages can begin with either right or left hands; whatever works best is the rule.

Notation

Rolls are not used to sustain notes unless specifically notated. The player controls any unwanted resonance with finger dampening or even a forearm pressed to the keyboard. The ringing sound of the bells is idiomatic to the instrument and though composers notate short durations, like the triangle, these are allowed to naturally decay.

Glockenspiel

Mallet Exercises I
Scales and Arpeggios

Siwe

Glockenspiel

Mallet Exercises II

Siwe

Double Stops

Glockenspiel

Mallet Chops

Siwe

poco a poco accelerando al fine

Fine

Glockenspiel

Siwe

Blue Funk

Glockenspiel

Latin Island

Siwe

Glockenspiel

Minor Swing

Siwe

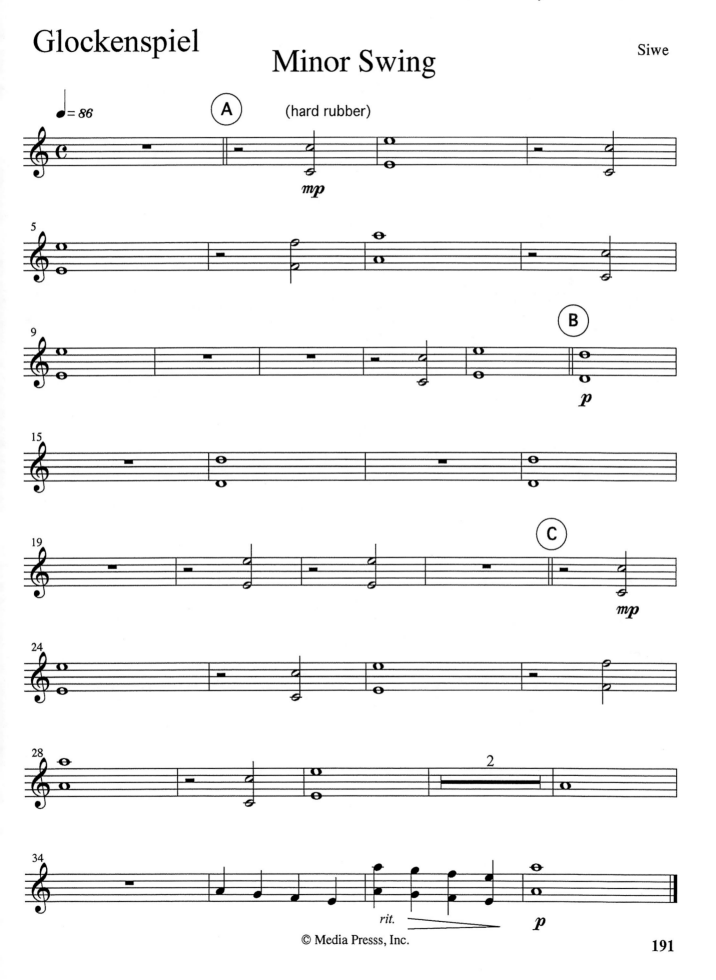

Bells

Siwe's Shuffle

Siwe

Glockenspiel

Straight Rock

Siwe

Tubular Bells
(tubular chimes)

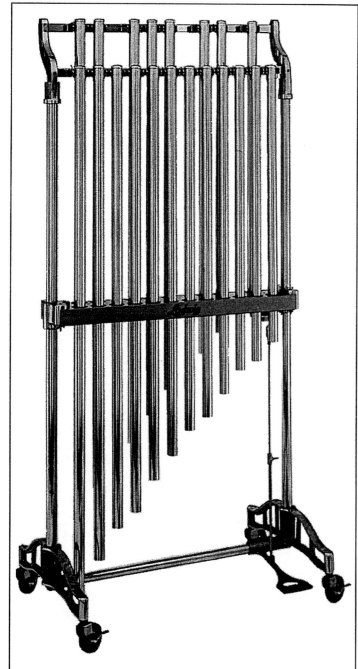

History

Tubular bells are "...a modern substitute for real bells..." (Marcuse 1964, 548). Always a poor imitation of the real thing (but much more practical), tubular bells "were introduced by John Hampton of Coventry in 1885" (Blades 1970, 401) for the peal of four bells in Sullivan's *The Golden Legend*. Nineteenth century opera and orchestra composers sometimes notated bell parts in bass clef which necessitated the construction of chime tubes of enormous length requiring the player to use a ladder. Occasionally real bells can be used if only one or two pitches are required, as in Berlioz' *Symphonie fantastique* (1830). Tubular chimes are constructed from brass tubes of one to two inches in diameter. Near the top of each tube a metal 'plug' is inserted to reinforce the area that is struck. Modern chime sets have a dampening mechanism worked by a pedal and are chrome plated to keep them from oxidizing.

Range

Sets of chimes used in the U.S. have a chromatic range of one octave plus a perfect fourth, notated c1 to f2. The instrument sounds one octave higher, though many people perceive them to sound lower. "One of the interesting characteristics of chimes is that there is no mode of vibration with a frequency at or even near, the pitch of the strike tone one hears. This is an example of a subjective tone created in the auditory system." (Rossing 1982, 42). There are so many works that call for notes outside the standard range that renting extra chimes has become common. As with bells and xylophones, playing passages an octave lower, or higher, is acceptable as long as the shape of the phrase is given consideration.

Mallets/Grip

Chime mallets are made from rolled rawhide, or today, a plastic/synthetic material. They are the same mallets common to metal workshops and can be purchased at your local hardware store. One grips them as though you would a hammer.

Playing Area/Tone Production/Stance

Tubular bells are always struck on the 'striking cap' at the very top of the tube. The action is a straight into-the-tube stroke that allows the hammer head to freely rebound. The upper arm does most of the work, with little, or no wrist action. Avoid striking the tubes at an angle. This causes unwanted harmonics and a weak sound.

It is important that the player position the bells and the music stand so that the conductor is visible.

Sticking

Most chime passages move slowly with few exceptions. This allows the player to play adjacent notes using the same mallet and to dampen the tubes by hand. Scale exercises that allow players to hand-dampen each note following the one struck are useful in perfecting this technique.

Notation

Rolls are not used to sustain notes. The ringing sound of the bells is idiomatic to the instrument, but care has to be taken that unwanted dissonance is not caused by the tubes' capability to resonate for a great length of time.

Tubular Bells

Mallet Exercises I

Scales and arpeggios

Siwe

Chimes

Mallet Exercises II

Siwe

Double Stops

Fine

D.C. al Fine

Tubular Bells

Mallet Chops

Siwe

poco a poco accelerando al fine

Fine

Chimes

Blue Funk

Siwe

Tubular Bells

Latin Island

Siwe

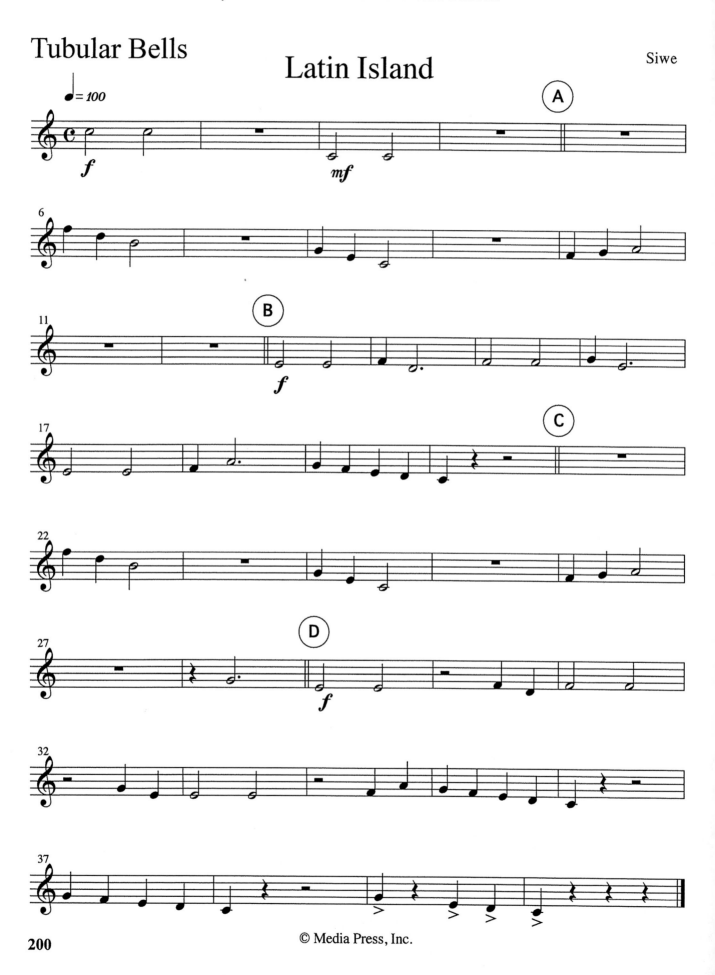

Tubular Bells

Minor Swing

Siwe

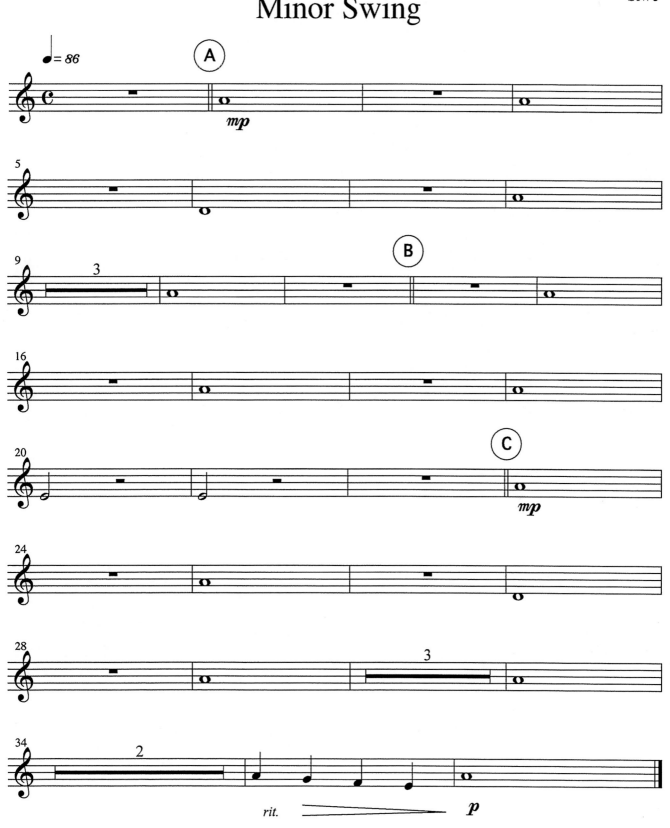

Chimes

Siwe's Shuffle

Siwe

202

Chimes

Straight Rock

Siwe

Vibraphone
(vibraharp)

History

In the mid-1920s, the motorized, aluminum bar 'vibraharp' was introduced by the Chicago based J.C. Deagan Co. Earlier, a rival company, Leedy Manufacturing of Indianapolis had produced the 'vibraphone,' an adapted version of an existing steel bar marimba. The design produced by Deagan beat out the rival Leedy adaptation, but the Leedy name 'vibraphone' has become the name most often used to identify this unique instrument. Early radio shows and recordings of the '20s helped promote the vibraphone, then perceived as a novelty instrument. Later a number of jazz band leaders, such as Adrian Rollini and Benny Goodman, saw the potential of the vibraphone adding it to their popular ensembles. Artists, such as Terri Gibbs and Lionel Hampton and later, Milt Jackson and Gary Burton, made today's vibraphone the most widely recognized mallet-keyboard percussion instrument and a staple of today's jazz orchestras and combos. The vibraphone has changed little since the first Deagan design. The bars are "made from a half-hard tempered-aluminum alloy". (Beck 1995, 340). They are suspended over metal resonators that contain rotating disks near the top. A multi-speed motor turns the disks, or baffles, creating a fluctuation of intensity perceived by the ear as a vibrato. A foot pedal operates a dampening bar stretching across the length of the instrument, allowing the player to let the bars resonate. To dampen individual notes, players must use their mallet heads or finger tips. An electronic vibraphone has been available commercially since the 1960s.

Range

The range of the most popular vibraphone model is three octaves, f to f3. There are a number of older and newer model vibraphones that extend the range a few notes both higher and lower, but the three octave model dominates the international market.

Mallets

Vibraphone mallets are similar to those used on the marimba. In fact, yarn-covered marimba mallets are often employed on the vibraphone. Professionals prefer cord-wound mallets or mallet heads wrapped with a fine gauge yarn. Mallet shafts can be made from rattan (preferred), birch or plastic. They vary little in length (9" to 15").

Grip

The grip used for vibraphone mallets is very similar to that used for holding snare drum sticks. Grasp the mallet shaft about one-third the distance from the end using the thumb and index finger. Wrap the other fingers lightly around the shaft. Both hands are the same. Do not grip the shaft too tightly; use just enough pressure to keep the mallet from slipping. Next, hold the mallets out over the keyboard, relax and drop the upper arms next to the body. Your wrists and hands should turn naturally, with the knuckles facing slightly upward, allowing for a smooth up-and-down wrist motion.

Three- and Four-Mallet Grips

Many beginning vibraphone parts exploit the sustaining possibilities of the instrument. Double stops and three, or four-note chords are common. The simple cross grip is the easiest for beginning players. See **Marimba** for details.

Use of the Pedal

If possible, the pedal should be depressed at the attack of a chord or notes of long duration. It should be released to dampen the sound at the very end of the written note value. If the passage has many notes of short duration, it is common to not use the pedal which, if depressed, would cause the notes to 'blur'. The exception would be when the composer desires this effect. With the pedal depressed, it is possible to allow some notes to ring out and others to be dampened. This is best accomplished by the technique of 'mallet dampening'. To mallet dampen a single resonating note, the player softly presses the mallet head into the middle of the bar.

Playing Area/Tone Production/Stance

For the best tone quality, vibraphone bars are struck in the center. The stroke used is an up-and-down wrist action. There is very little natural rebound off the bars; the player must lift the mallet head quickly away from the bar to insure a resonant tone. The need to keep either the right or left foot on the pedal restricts the players movement along the length of the keyboard. One step, either right or left, helps position them in front of bars that are being played. It is important that the player stand erect and avoid bending over the bars. Also, avoid crowding the keyboard. Keep the body at a distance that allows the player to reach the center of the accidentals and natural keys with ease.

Sticking

Beginning players must be taught to alternate right and left hands as much as possible, even though simple parts are sometimes playable with just one mallet. Practicing scales and arpeggios is helpful in learning how to cross over and under to reach adjacent notes. Doubling notes, i.e., playing two adjacent notes with one hand, is more common to the vibraphone than to the wooden keyboard instruments. Passages can begin with either right or left hands; whatever works best is the rule.

Notation

To sustain notes on the vibraphone, the player uses the pedal. Rolls are not used to sustain notes unless specifically notated.

Vibraphone

Mallet Exercises I

Siwe

Scales and Arpeggios

© Media Press, Inc.

Vibraphone

Mallet Exercises II

3-note chords

Siwe

Fine

D.C. al Fine

Vibraphone

Mallet Chops

Siwe

poco a poco accelerando al fine

Fine

© Media Press, Inc.

Vibraphone

Blue Funk

Siwe

Vibraphone

Latin Island

Siwe

Vibraphone

Minor Swing

Siwe

Vibraphone

Siwe's Shuffle

Siwe

Vibraphone

Straight Rock

Siwe

Mallet Test Pieces

Siwe

(Mallet Test Pieces, p. 2)

Siwe

The Drum Set

History:

"The drum set, a twentieth-century creation, is the most ubiquitous percussion instrument in American culture today. It is an instrument, which has been, and continues to be, subjected to a dynamic, evolving process." (Pollack 2000, 3) The originators of the 'drum set' were percussionists. They were part of brass bands popular in the late nineteenth and early twentieth centuries. For a variety of reasons, some economic, drummers in these early bands developed a style of 'double drumming' where one player could perform on both the bass drum and snare drum. To free their hands in order to play more complicated figures on the snare drum, e.g., rolls, enterprising drummers developed various foot-operated devices to play the bass drum parts. Mounting a cymbal on top of the bass drum and striking it with the other cymbal also reduced the need for an additional player. With a cymbal in one hand, the player struck the mounted cymbal. The hand cymbal was quickly pulled back, allowing the plates to ring. Often the player would intentionally dampen both, 'choking' the sound. Later, another foot operated device, the 'hi-hat,' would better serve this purpose and soon become a standard drum set part along with a 'ringing,' suspended cymbal. In addition to these basic percussion instruments (bass drum, snare drum and cymbals), early band percussionists were expected to play various sound effects such as Chinese blocks, bird and train whistles, etc., known in the trade as 'traps.' In fact, another name for the drum set is the 'trap set.' The evolution to a single set of drums (bass drum, tom-toms, snare drum, hi-hat and suspended cymbals) was driven by the various styles of music played by dance bands and theater orchestras throughout the twentieth century. Any history of the drum set goes hand in hand with the needs of drummers who played dixieland, swing, bebop, hard bop, cool jazz, rock and fusion.

Drum Set Components:

Snare drum & stand - The marching snare was replaced early on by a smaller, orchestral drum laid upon a chair or cradled in a stand. Today's drum set snare drum is secured on an adjustable stand specifically designed for it. Since the player is seated, the snare drum stand must be able to be positioned low enough to accommodate this height.

Bass drum & pedal - The large concert bass drums and the smaller marching versions used during the early days of Dixieland have evolved into a 22 or 24 inch diameter drum with a foot pedal attached on the playing side. Since the drum tends to move forward from the blows of the pedal, two spurs mounted on the drum are needed to keep it in place. Wooden floors (e.g. school gymnasiums) suffer from the sharp spurs, so most drummers carry a piece of thick rug to help prevent any damage.

Hi-hat & cymbals - An early version of the hi-hat mounted two opposing cymbals on a spring-loaded foot operated device. The cymbals were close to the floor, about one foot, and the device was referred to as the 'low boy,' or 'low hat'. In 1927 a version very similar to today's was developed that

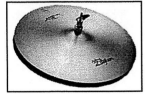

raised the cymbals high enough so that the player could strike them with sticks or use the pedal to crash them together. The hi-hat used by contemporary drummers has a substantial foot pedal and, like the bass drum, a much needed set of spurs to keep it in place. Cymbals are now made specifically for use on the hi-hat. The lower cymbal is slightly heavier than the top one and sits on a small, felt-covered platform attached to an adjustable pole. The top cymbal is held in place by an attachment called the 'hi-hat clutch.' The cymbals are placed between two felt insulating washers mounted on the center rod and held in position by a thumb screw device. It is important that the correct amount of tension be applied to the hi-hat clutch so that the top cymbal is secure, yet still resonates when struck. A popular size for a hi-hat cymbal is 14 inches in diameter.

Ride & crash cymbals - The cymbal first suspended on top of the marching bass drum evolved into one suspended on its own pole. Early drummers used existing cymbals, both Turkish and Chinese, to add color to their drum sets. Later they were used for keeping time and for solo breaks. Small 'splash' cymbals provided accents, larger ones were used to 'ride the time.' A basic drum set cymbal array needs at least two suspended cymbals, one 'crash' or 'splash' for accents and one 'ride' for basic time keeping. Important to the sound of a suspended cymbal is a good floor stand, or cymbal pole. In order to avoid any extraneous noise factors, the cymbal must be well insulated from the pole with felt washers and rubber tubing. As with the hi-hats, the amount of tension securing the cymbal needs proper attention so as not to stifle the sound.

Tom-toms - The Chinese tom-toms used by early drum set players have been replaced with tunable toms that range in size from 6 inches in diameter to 16 inches. A complete drum set needs at least two toms of differing sizes, a small tom mounted in front of the snare drum and a floor tom that is placed to the drummer's side.

Drum thrones - Positioning the drummer behind the drum set so that all the components are comfortably within reach is very important. A strong, easily-adjusted drum stool, or 'throne,' is absolutely necessary. Money spent on a quality drum throne will help insure the health and safety of the players who use it.

Drum Set Exercises

Repeat each 1 or 2 bar figure until you can play it with ease. Use the metronome to help keep time.

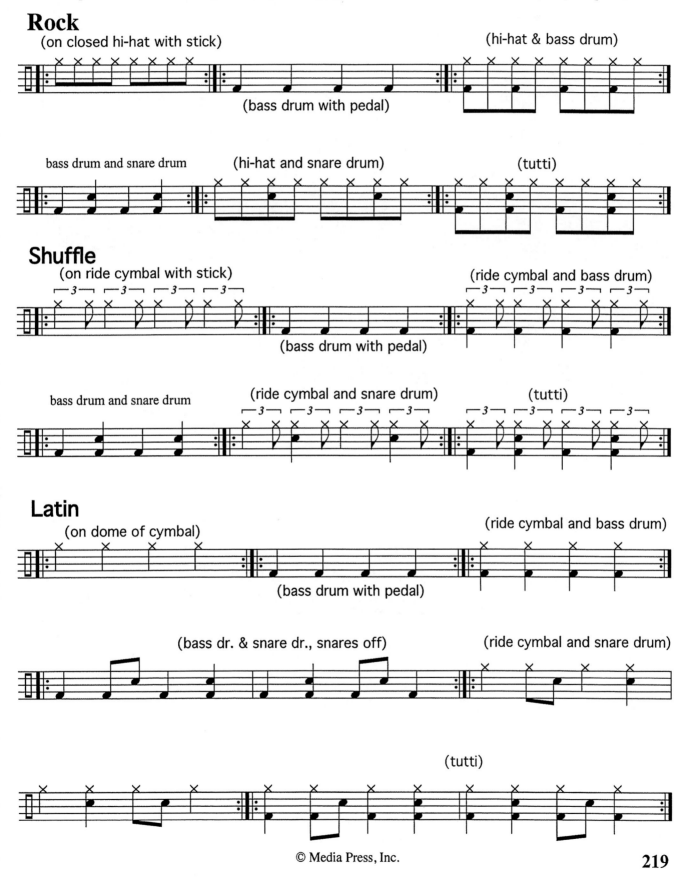

Swing

Funk

Sample Drum Chart

BLUE FUNK

SIWE

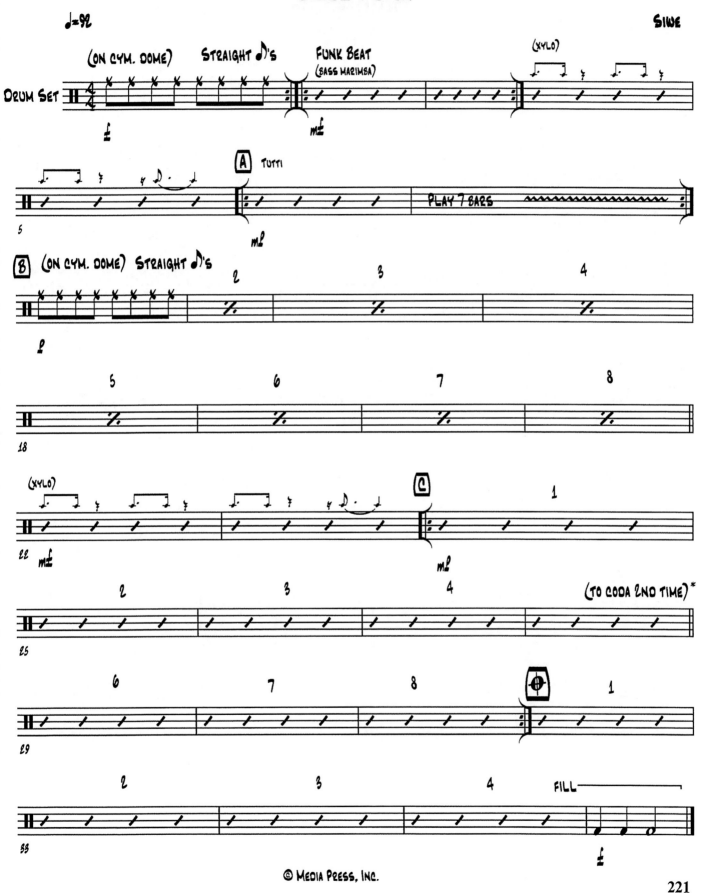

Drum Set

Blue Funk

Siwe

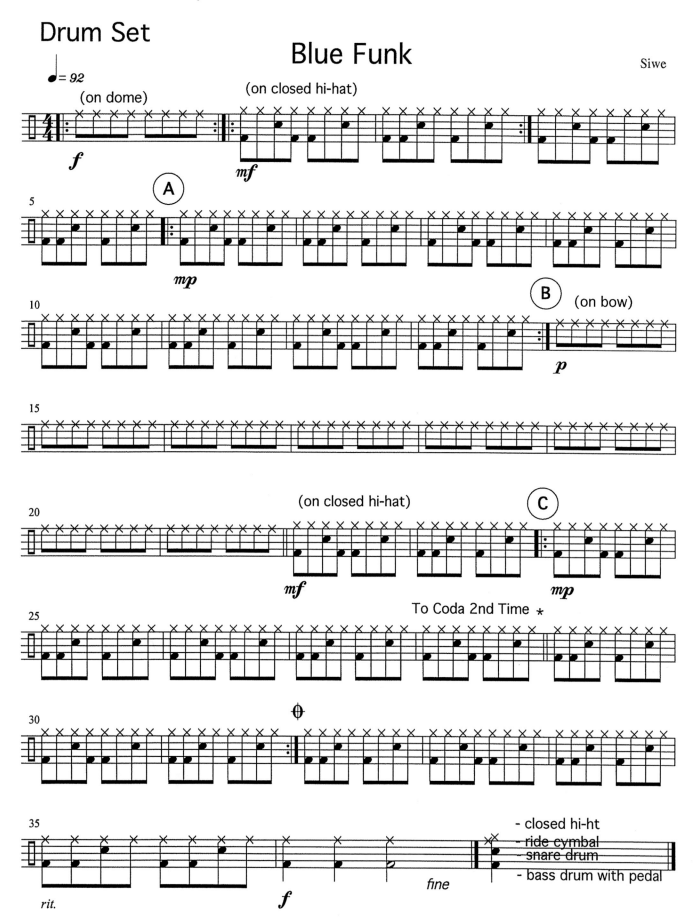

© Media Press, Inc.

Latin Island

Drum Set

Siwe

Drum Set
(swing dotted rhythms)

Minor Swing

Siwe

© Media Presss, Inc.

Siwe's Shuffle

Drum Set

Siwe

225

Drum Set

Straight Rock

Siwe

Rattles and Shakers
(Maracas, Cabaça, etc.)

History
Maracas are shakers made from hollowed gourds filled with seeds and have handles attached. They are thought to have originated amongst the Indians of South America (Marcuse 1964, 330). Composer Edgard Varèse calls for high and low maracas in his 1931 work *Ionisation*. Other shakers include the Brazilian *caxixi*, a small woven basket filled with seeds and used to accompany the berimbau. The *chocalho* and *ganza*, two tube-shaped instruments made of metal, bamboo, plastic or gourd are, like most shakers, filled with pellets, stones or seeds. An example of scoring for *ganza* can be found in Villa-Lobos' *Bachianas Brasileiras No. 2 (1933)*. There are a few shakers, both African and Latin-American that have a netting of beads woven around the outside of the instrument. The Brazilian *cabaça* (or *afoxé*) is made from a hollow, grooved coconut shell with a "netting of seeds called a lagima da nossa sehora (Holy Mother's tears)". (Beck 1995, 160).

The *quijada del burro* is a unique rattle made from the jawbone of a burro. Taken from burro carcasses found bleached clean in the deserts of the southwest and Mexico, these instruments were brightly painted and decorated with small pellet bells. Held at the point where the jaws unite, the rattle is struck with a closed fist making the bells and teeth rattle. With the coming of the automobile, the source of burro jawbones has disappeared and the instrument has been replaced by the *vibraslap*. John Cage calls for a *quijada* in his percussion ensemble work *Third Construction* (1941).

Performance Techniques
The seed, or pellet filled shakers are most often used to play ostinato rhythmic lines. A combined wrist and arm motion that produces an even pulse with periodic accents offers the best results without creating fatigue for the player. To play soft, distinct rhythmic groups, the player uses a short, downward wrist action, causing all the interior seeds to strike together.

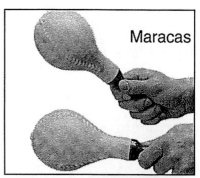
Maracas

Cabaça

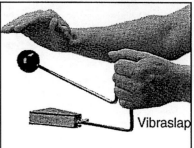
Vibraslap

Caxixi

Chocalho

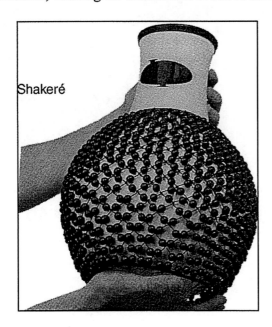
Shakeré

Scrapers and Raspers
(Güiro, reco-reco, etc.)

History
Scrapers were "found in paleolithic and neolithic Europe" (Marcuse 1964, 464). Made from wood, bone, shell, gourd or other material, scrapers and raspers have been found throughout world cultures. Sometimes solid, often hollow, they usually have carved, transverse grooves that are scraped with a wood, bone or metal rod creating a sharp, penetrating sound. Composers sometimes use this "rasping" sound for its unique timbre as in Stravinsky's *Le sacre du printemps (1913),* but most often it carries folkloristic implications.

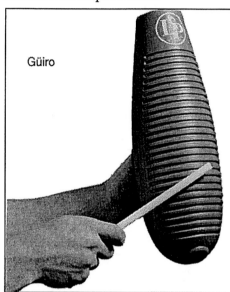

Güiro

Made from a hollowed, grooved gourd, "the *güiro* is one of the instruments most closely associated with Latin music." (Beck 1995, 233). A version made from metal is called the *güira*. The Brazilian *reco-reco* is made from bamboo "with transverse notches, or a small metal box, etc., scraped with a small stick" (Marcuse 1964, 440).

Performance Techniques
Techniques differ slightly with each instrument in this family group. For the güiro, grasp the instrument with one hand at the finger holes carved in its back. You can either hold the güiro upright as pictured, or horizontally. The scraping stick is held as you would a snare drum stick. Scrape the notches lightly, with a quick motion, regardless of the note duration. If the tempo becomes too fast for this technique, just tap the gourd with a single stroke. A typical güiro pattern involves a single scraped note followed by two taps, i.e. scrape-tap-tap, scrape-tap-tap, etc..

Agogo

History
Double bells were introduced into the New World from Africa. They consist of two single, clapperless bells connected by a common handle. Usually made of metal, the two bells always differ in pitch and are struck with a wood stick or metal rod. The Afro-Brazilian double bell, the agogô, was "used in voodoo rites in Rio, Bahia, and Pernambuco." (Marcuse 1964, 7).

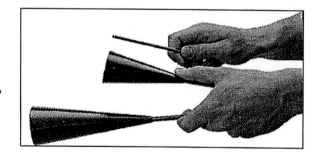

Bongo Drums

History
Bongo is a "Cuban term for a variety of small Afro-Cuban drums." (Marcuse 1964, 61). A popular version in the West comprises two tunable, single-headed drums. Percussionists favor the bongos finding them useful in an array of graduated tom-toms. Composers have used the drums for their unique timbre as did Varèse in his 1931 *Ionisation*, but more often score them for their ethnic flavor as did Bernstein in the 1957 *West Side Story*.

Originally goat-skin heads were tacked on to the bongo wooden shells, and players used heat from an open fire to remove excess moisture, carefully raising the pitch to the desired tone. Today's drums are tunable and players use small wrenches to tighten and loosen the heads. It is important to keep skin-headed drums away from extreme heat and to loosen their heads after use and before long storage periods. For school use it may be advisable to use synthetic heads on your bongos and congas.

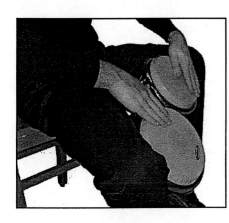

Playing Techniques
Bongos are traditionally played with hands rather than mallets or sticks. Players are seated holding the bongo between their knees with the bongo heads at a forward angle. Various sounds are created by how and where a player strikes the head. For concert use in school bands, it may be advisable to mount the bongos on an adjustable stand with the player using rubber covered mallets. This technique is popular with Caribbean bands and helps with balance and articulation problems. It also helps to prevent injury to the hands and fingers of young players.

Conga Drum

History and Performance Techniques
The conga drum is "perhaps the most important instrument in Afro-Cuban music". (Beck 1995, 231). It also refers to a dance or song. The drums come in three sizes. The smallest is called the *quinto*; the middle drum the *conga;* and the large drum *tumba*, or *tumbadora*. To play the drums as a professional would play them, one must master a number of hand strokes that produce muted and open tones, high penetrating slaps and low resonant bass notes. A basic conga pattern in Latin music is the *tumbao* that incorporates all the above sounds over a steady pulse. The congas have found their way into both popular and art music. Gershwin called for congas in his opera *Porgy and Bess* (1935).

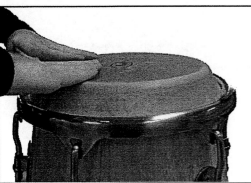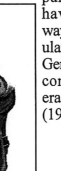

Basic Hand Position

Etude for Latin Instruments

Siwe

Guiro

Etude for Latin Instruments

Siwe

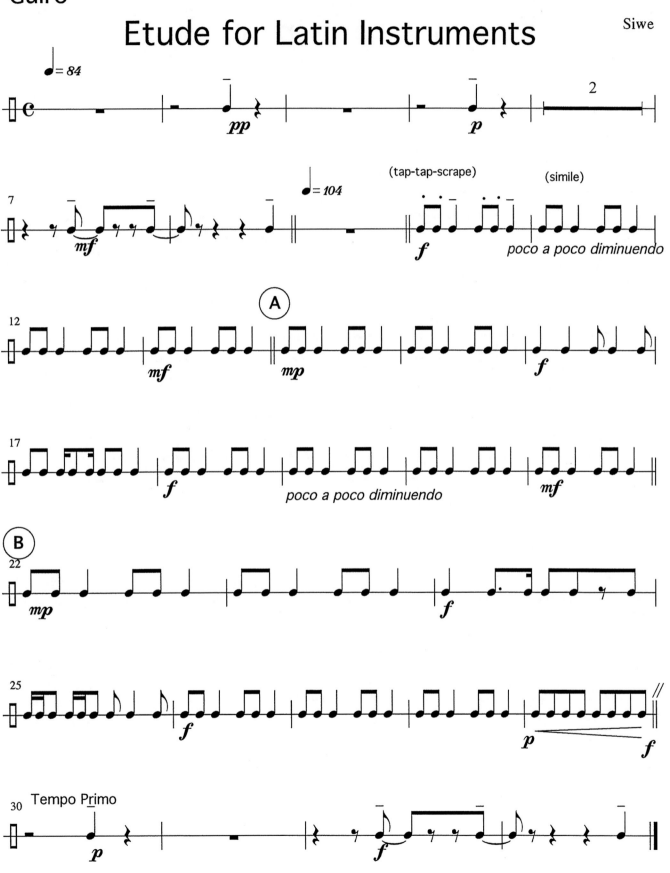

Etude for Latin Instruments

Siwe

Etude for Latin Instruments

Siwe

Etude for Latin Instruments

Bongos

Siwe

234   © Media Press, Inc.

Conga

Etude for Latin Instruments

Siwe

Marching Percussion

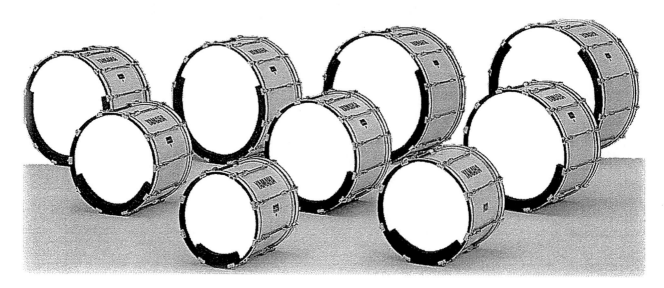

History: Seen on ancient Sumerian reliefs, drums were noted as early as 2500 B.C. Evidence that people actually marched with them dates from about 1600 B.C. How marching percussion evolved is a story whose thread weaves across continents and ages. "The use of drums and bells for signaling and giving orders... is attested to in China from at least the 7th century B.C." (New Grove, 2nd Ed.). "As early as Virgil's Aeneid (3 B.C.) the sound of (percussion) instruments was acknowledged as a means of exciting ardour in advancing armies" (New Grove, 2nd Ed.). Marching percussion's history begins with its use by the armies of ancient Europe, Asia and Africa. Trumpets and drums were part of the Janissary bands of the Ottoman Sultans. The influence of this 'Turkish music' on Western culture is well documented, but how the music sounded is unknown. How early marching percussion was used is better documented. Swiss and German mercenaries in the early Renaissance used fife and drums "as an aid to marching in step.." (New Grove, 2nd Ed.). "By the 17th century European armies distinguished between two types of musical units, the 'field music' and the 'band of music'." (New Grove, 2nd Ed.). The former sounded signals and commands for the troops; the latter played for ceremonial and social functions. British marching bands of mixed winds and percussion (and the Scottish bagpipe and drum units) were the early models for marching percussion in colonial America. By the time of the American Revolution, trumpets and drums were an integral part of the military, providing a voice of communication between the commanders and their troops. Bands of trumpets and drums aided in the training of troops, helping them to march together, signaling when they should attack or retreat, alerting them to enemy movement and, in general, serving to control them both on the battle field and in camp, from 'reveille' to 'tattoo.'

The early drum manuals were not notated, but the beating patterns were described. An English-born U.S. Marine, Charles Stewart Ashworth, was one of the first to notate the basic patterns (or rudiments), used by drummers during the time of the American Revolution. During the American Civil War, authors Bruce and Emmett continued this tradition. Even the famous band master, John Philip Sousa, contributed a book for trumpets and drums. In 1872 a national organization sanctioned field competition for drum and bugle corps. In the 1920s and '30s, various American Legion and VFW posts throughout the U.S. sponsored drum and bugle corps for young boys. These competitions were local, regional and national, and later included solo competition as well.

In an attempt to standardize the rudimental patterns used by the corps, a group of prominent drummers met in 1933 and formed the National Association of Rudimental Drummers (NARD). The 26 drum patterns they selected became the standard for competition evaluation. After WW II, the VFW and American Legion sponsorships waned. Marching bands and drum corps moved away from the military style of music. In 1957 Remo Belli introduced plastic drum heads making outdoor performances much less dependent on weather conditions. Other drum innovations and inventions continued through the 1950s and '60s with some bands adding marching timpani, bells and xylophones. New sanctioning bodies formed (DCA - 1963, DCI-1971) helping to promote marching percussion. The drum carrier was introduced in the mid-1970s allowing drummers to discard the drum sling and use the matched grip. In the 1980s the Percussive Arts Society revised the snare drum rudiments, adding many new patterns and regrouping them into more understandable categories. The 'pit' was introduced into drum and bugle competition allowing unlimited use of mallet-keyboard instruments, timpani and auxiliary percussion. Today's school marching programs reflect their military heritage as well as recent trends introduced by today's drum and bugle corps. How and to what degree music educators incorporate past traditions and recent trends depends on the needs of their program. A recommended approach is outlined in the following material.

Philosophy: The overall guiding concept or principle that applies to drum lines is <u>uniformity</u>. A marching percussion presentation must be well-balanced and well-proportioned, exact and precise, both aurally and visually. The precision that your drum line brings to the field will effect the entire band. Without a well-drilled and sonically sound drum corps, it will be impossible for any band to have the necessary visual symmetry, or smoothness of movement and flow, nor to march together to a steady beat. The concept of uniformity applies to all areas except the percussion pit, where just about anything goes and you are limited only by your creativity.

Equipment: It is almost impossible to reach visual uniformity or sameness of sound with equipment that differs in quality and brand type. To begin with, it is recommended that you invest in equipment that is designed for field use. Using concert instruments on the field is not a good idea! They are not designed to withstand the physical wear and tear. This caveat includes <u>never</u> <u>using</u> <u>concert instruments</u> <u>in</u> <u>the</u> <u>pit</u>, if you decide to incorporate such a group into your field band program.

<u>Snare drums:</u> 14" diameter, 12" depth. The current popular sound for marching snare drums is an extremely high sound, designed to cut through the texture of the band and the other percussion instruments. Tuning the drums so that each drum matches is important. The extreme pressure caused by tuning the drum can cause heads to break and shells to collapse. Tune according to the drum manufacturers' recommendations, using a torque wrench with a gauge to insure evenness of tension. Be sure the drums have

'feet' so that when they are placed on the ground during rest periods, the heads will not come into contact with anything that would cause them to break. Even better, make a rule that the drums are to be placed on their sides when not in use. Use nylon-tipped snare sticks, quality drum carriers that are fully adjustable, and remember to dress the snare drum line through the bodies, not the drums. Since your population (ages 10 - 17) is in its growing period, remember to place the students with regard to height. Always remember, uniformity is your guiding principle.

<u>Tenor drums:</u> 8", 10", 12", 14" quad arrays. Tune the heads about a minor third apart. Each drum should be tightened evenly and almost to the maximum or highest pitch possible. Carriers mounted with 4 drums are quite heavy. It is important to select players for these positions who are able to physically

handle the load. The tenor drum sticks should have small heads and be taped with the same color tape that you use for the snare and bass drum sticks. Again, differences in colors of wood distract from the uniformity that you are trying to create. Taping the sticks with white (or colored) tape is recommended. The tenors need a pair of soft sticks for parts orchestrated with exposed rolls.

<u>Bass drums:</u> 20", 22", 24" (optional - 18", 26") Marching bass drums need inside tone controls to dampen the harmonics and give the drum a more focused sound. Beaters should be matched to the size of the drum as with all other percussion instruments. One of the bass drums should be tuned to have a 'low, booming sound'. The highest drum should be tightened so that you can roll on the drum. As with the tenors, tune the bass drums so that they are approximately a minor third apart.

<u>Cymbals:</u> When selecting cymbals, it is recommended that you select heavy weight cymbals, with the diameter as large as the players can handle. Depending upon your age group. the cymbals can range from 16' to 22' in diameter. Cymbal players must use gloves and cymbal pads to protect their hands.

Uniformity: A uniform approach to playing the various instruments that make up the drum line is obviously important. Sticking for the snare drums must be the same. To help develop uniformity of technique, you should utilize exercises that will enable you to spot style discrepancies. The snare drummers must select either 'matched grip' or 'traditional grip'. It is impossible to obtain the necessary symmetry with a mix of two playing styles. Striking area, hand and arm movements, the distance the snare bead moves, etc., all should be exactly the same. The same details need to be addressed for the tenors, bass drum and cymbal players.

The music, marching formations and drum cadences that they must learn are a lot to expect from young players. I recommend that the percussion section have its own warm-ups, separate from the band, and that additional, or separate, rehearsal time be required for the entire unit. Have the drum line learn the rhythms first; add the dynamics later.

Instrumentation: Utilize at least 3 bass drums. To obtain the necessary balance use twice as many snare drums as tenor drums and half as many cymbal players as tenor drummers.

Marching and Drill Formations: Whether on parade or on the field, it is best to have the strong players in the center of the lines. All of them should know that they must listen to the player behind them and that the rear positioned players follow the conductor. When charting the movements of the various instruments, remember that it is difficult to turn quickly and movements to the side look sloppy. If the cymbals are to be played with snare sticks, the snare drummers need to be charted so they are in close proximity. Keeping the entire drum line near the front of all formations will help you to avoid sound phasing and other unwanted coordination problems, but you may create a balance problem.

Snare Drum

Siwe

Marching Roll Development

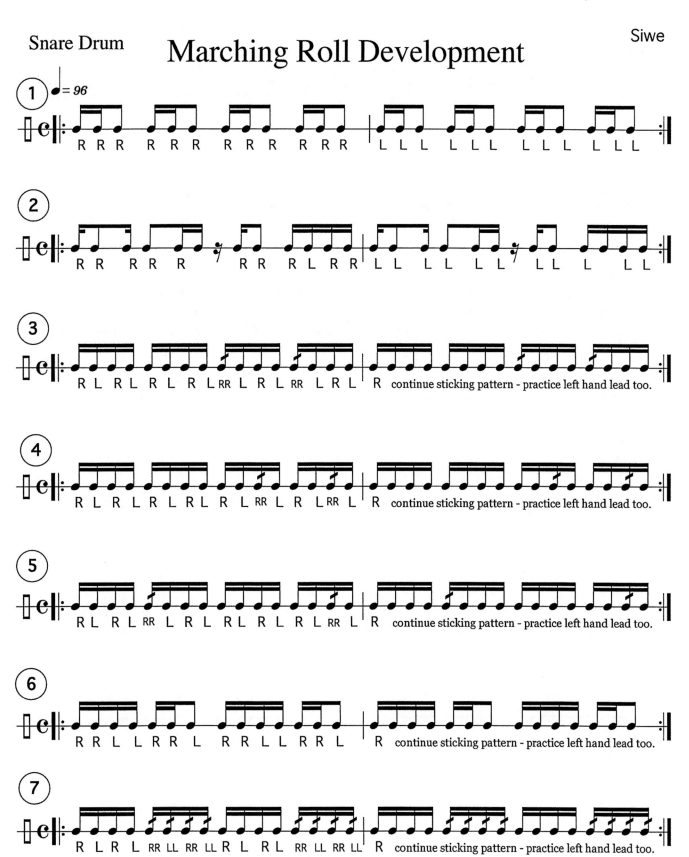

Snare Drum

Marching Warm-ups

(-even taps-)

Siwe

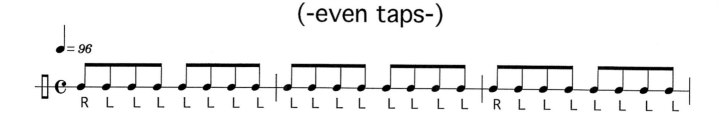

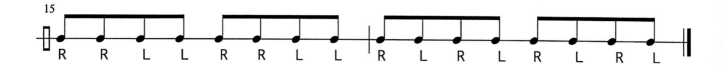

Quad Toms

Marching Warm-ups

(-even taps-)

Siwe

Cymbals

Marching Warm-ups

(-even taps-)

Siwe

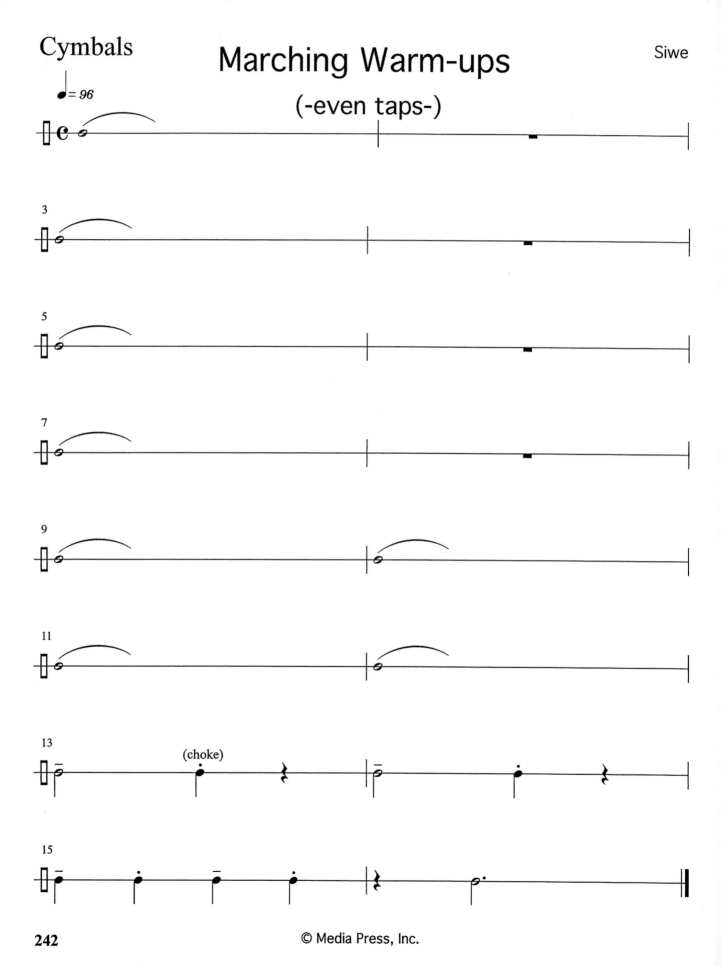

Bass Drums

- High
- Medium
- Low

Marching Warm-ups

Siwe

(-even taps-)

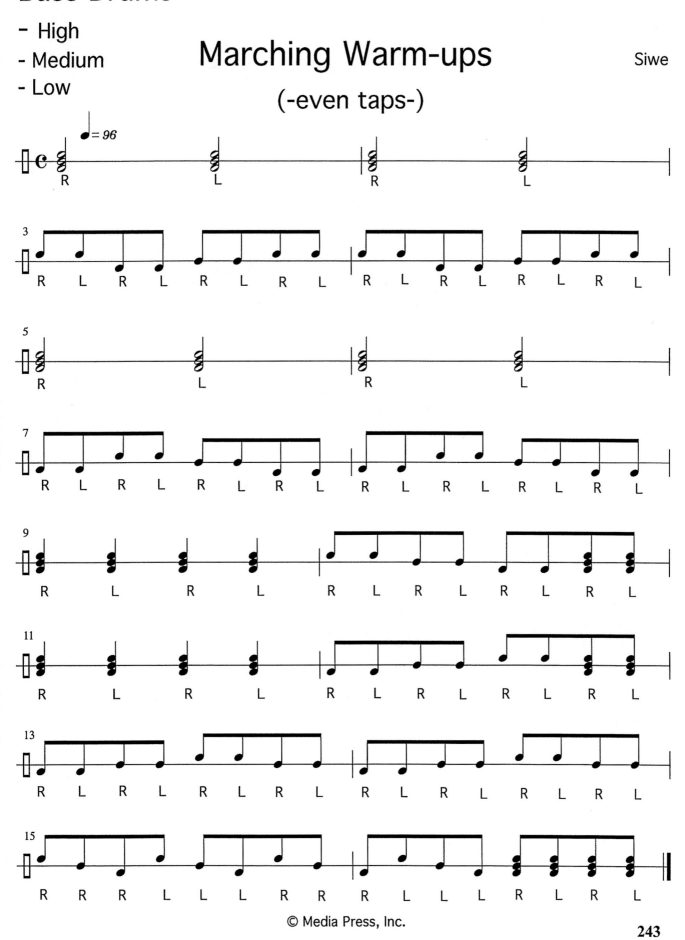

Snare Drums

Marching Warm-ups

Siwe

(- with accents -)

Quad Toms

Siwe

Marching Warm-ups
(- with accents -)

Percussion: A Course of Study for the Future Band and Orchestra Director

Marching Warm-ups
(- with accents -)

Cymbals

Siwe

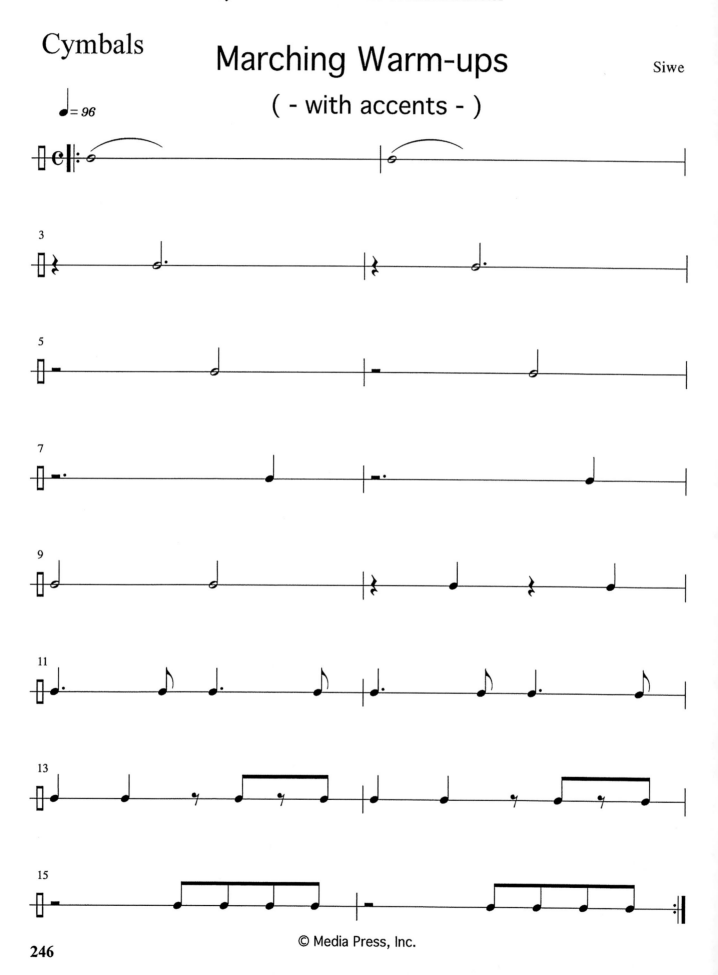

Marching Warm-ups
(- with accents -)

Bass Drums - H M L

Siwe

Snare Drums

Corps Style Cadences

Siwe

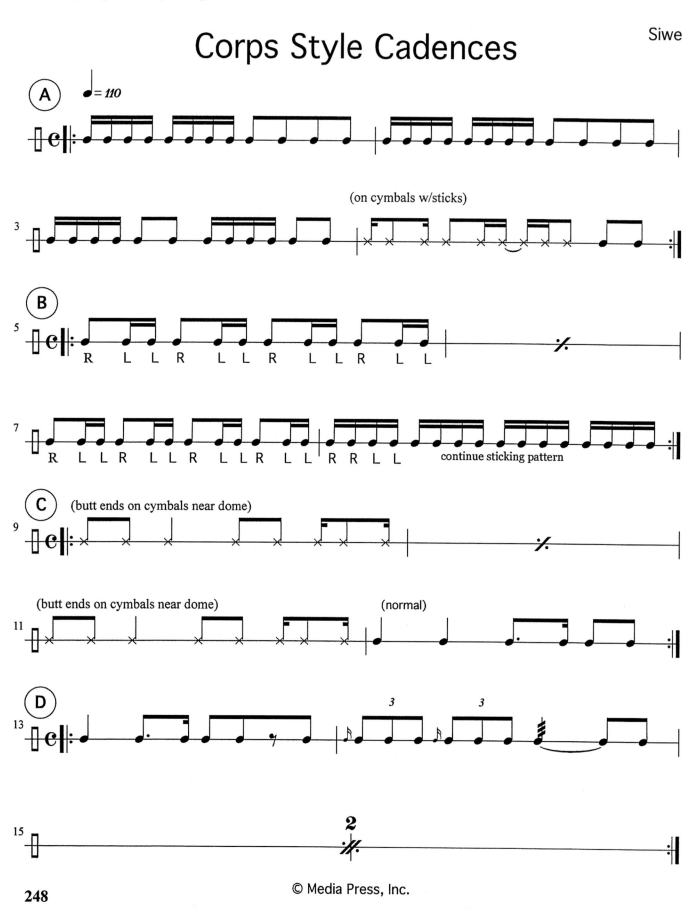

Quad Toms

Corps Style Cadences

Siwe

Cymbals

Corps Style Cadences

Siwe

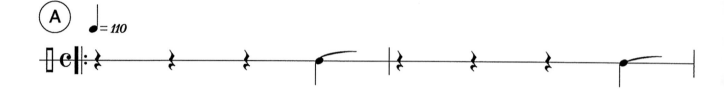

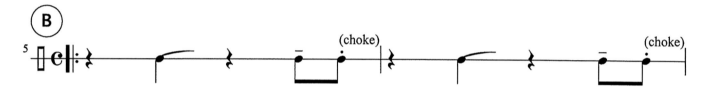

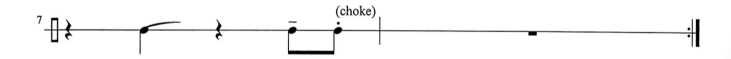

Bass Drums-M

Corps Style Cadences

Siwe

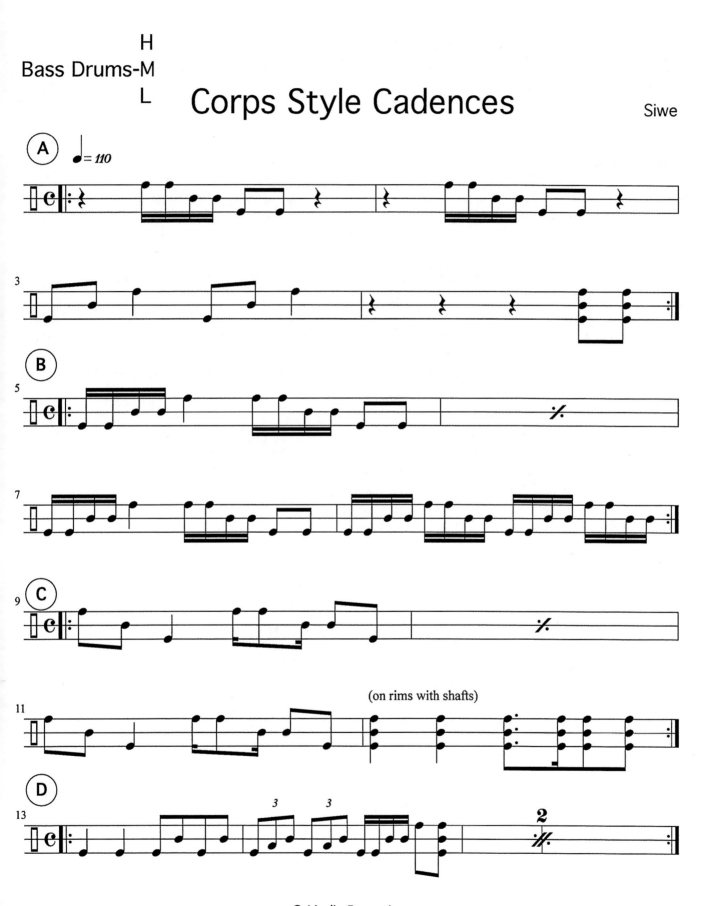

(on rims with shafts)

Care and Repair
Snare Drums, Bass Drums, Bongos, etc.

<u>All Drums</u>: Check plastic heads for dents and wear. Replace broken and worn heads. Clean heads with detergent and warm water.

<u>Bass Drum</u>: With the head off, clean grit and dirt from under counter hoops with soap and water. Remove paper spitballs, gum and other unwanted material. Lightly oil tension rods and tighten all nuts and bolts, inside and outside of the shells.

Problem: Rattles in bass drum. Solution: Remove one head. Tighten all nuts and bolts and clean out interior of shell. Replace head and carefully adjust all tension rods. If some appear too loose, they may be the cause of your rattle. Placing small pieces of moleskin between the clamp and rim may help.

<u>Snare Drum</u>: Adjust snare mechanisms, clip off any loose snares with wire cutters and replace any snare release mechanisms that are beyond adjustment.

Problem: Snare will not stay in the 'on' position. Solution: Make sure snares are installed properly and centered across the snare head. Tighten (or loosen) snare tension adjustment a little at a time. Test after each adjustment until snare release operates correctly. Note: If drum is old, the cam may be worn out. If so, replace entire snare release mechanism.

<u>Skin Headed Drums</u>: Check calfskin, goat and other animal-hide heads for adequate collar. If little or no collar, wet head with damp cloth and tighten a small amount. After 24 hours, check for collar. If more is needed, repeat process. Too much collar can be reduced by again wetting the head. Then, loosen tension rods and allow to dry. The head will shrink. Repeat as needed.

Cymbals

<u>Cymbals</u>: Remove straps. Wash cymbals with strong detergent and warm water to remove unwanted grime and sticky material. If you like, the cymbals can be polished using any quality brass cleaner, though it would be for show purposes not as a needed care action. Check for small cracks. If they appear near the edge of the cymbal, it may be possible to repair. Otherwise, replace the cymbal.

Problem: Small crack at cymbal edge. Solution: Drill 1/16 inch hole at end of crack. Saw (or grind out) a small V-shaped section, removing the crack.

Cymbal Pads and Straps: Wipe grease from cymbal pads. Check cymbal straps for wear. Replace if necessary. Use the following visual guide to tie straps. Make sure the straps are securely knotted.

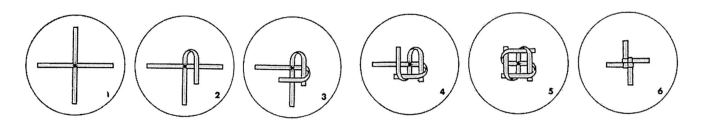

Timpani

Since plastic heads have almost totally replaced calfskin heads, most timpani head problems are now easy to diagnose and can be solved simply (i.e., no more problems with humidity and temperature sensitivity). Drums will stay trouble free for years if you: (1) tune each drum head to its recommended basic pitch; (2) lubricate the rim of the bowl and counter hoop area where the head touches; and (3) keep the correct amount of tension on the main spring and, if it has one, drum-key operated friction adjustment. In fact, the reliable, durable design of spring-action timpani fitted with plastic heads has led many to ignore timpani maintenance altogether; not a good idea.

Plastic timpani heads do develop dents, small cuts and tears often because the drums are used as tables or percussion carts. A partial solution is to make a set of covers from Masonite or thin plywood. Cover one side with a felt-like material and attach three to four straps with buckles to the other side. Make the straps long enough to pass through the tension rod area and secure the cover. You can print the head diameter (32", 29" etc.) on each cover to help identify the drums while in storage.

Once each year, remove the accumulation of dirt and grease from timpani heads using soap and hot water. If the head "creaks" or "squeaks" remove it. Clean and lubricate the rim and counter hoop, rotate the head and refit it to the drum. This is the point where most directors (and even many percussionists) lose confidence or are reluctant to take the time needed to go through what some believe to be a long and tedious procedure that might end with the drum sounding worse!

I recommend that on a standard set of four to five timpani, you replace a minimum of one head each year. Following the procedure outlined below, you will be able to remove and replace a head within an hour. You will also be able to tune and "clear" the head, improve its tone quality and return the drum to service quickly. Doing this at least once a year will keep the needed knowledge and skill at your fingertips so that if an emergency does occur you will be able to handle it with ease.

Equipment Needed: cleaning rags or paper towels, pipe cleaners, light oil, Teflon timpani tape, timpani stick, timpani key, snare drum key, small strobe or tuner.

Step One: Remove the old head carefully! Keep your foot on the pedal (lowest pitch position) as you use the timpani key to quickly loosen the tension rods by going around the drum a few turns at a time. When the tension is off, you can ease the pedal forward (as if raising the pitch). A few final turns will free the tension rods completely, then you can lift them, along with the counter hoop, and set everything aside. If the tension rods are "gritty", wipe the threads clean with a lightly-oiled rag. For the hard-to-reach threads of the kettle lug assembly, try using pipe cleaners. Clean the rim of the bowl and the counter hoop, using a damp rag (old-timers still use fine Emory cloth).

Step Two: Install the new head. Place a strip of Teflon tape over the bearing ridge of the bowl. Follow the application directions on the package. Carefully place (center) the new head onto the kettle, then place the counter hoop over the head. Take care that both hoop and head remain centered. Replace the tension rods using your fingers to thread them just enough to meet the counter hoop. With the timpani key, apply tension to each rod, one or two turns at a time. As tension increases, you can ease the task by using the foot pedal, returning it slowly to its beginning basic position. Use the stick to softly strike the head. If it resonates, thing are going well. If not, check to see if the head is still centered on the kettle. Continue to increase tension so that when the pedal is in its lowest position, the head is just below its lowest recommended basic pitch (see Timpani Range Chart for recommended lowest pitch).

Since you have never touched the master tension adjustment, your drum should now hold a pitch throughout its natural range of a perfect fifth (assuming it worked before you started the process). If the pedal slips producing a higher pitch, loosen the master spring a few turns; if it slips producing a lower pitch, apply tension. On those models with a friction adjustment, you can now use your snare drum key, inserting it in the hole near the pedal mechanism to apply just enough "brake" to make the pedal movement feel smooth, yet secure.

Step Three: Set the drum's pedal to a mid-range position and a recognizable pitch. Using the hand strobe, lightly strike the head at each post, adjusting slightly as needed. When all the posts are in tune, recheck the base pitch and adjust if necessary.

Daily Timpani Check!
1. Base Pitch - make sure drums are set to the recommended lowest pitch.
2. Pedal Action - make sure pedals move freely and hold on all pitches within the drum's range.
3. Clear heads, i.e., check all posts and adjust pitch if necessary.

Mallet-Keyboard Instruments

For mallet-keyboard instruments with plastic or wooden bars, remove dirt and sticky material using warm water, a mild detergent and a soft cloth. Dry wooden bars and apply a light coat of lemon oil. For metal bars, use strong detergent, warm water and a soft cloth to remove embedded dirt.

Check the bars' suspension cord for wear. Replace if necessary and readjust tension.

Straighten suspension posts (with keys removed) using chime hammer, and replace any worn or lost rubber insulators.

Biennially the bars should be checked using a strobe. If out of tune, send bars to reputable tuner.

Problem: Cracked wooden bar. Solution: Send bar to tuner; it may be reparable. If not, have tuner replace the bar. This is normally part of their service.

Remove resonators and clear unwanted materials from interior. Dust and replace.

Check wheels for wear. Clean and oil.

Make sure that the vibraphone motor pulley is still in place. Lightly oil rotating baffles at friction points.

Problem: Vibe notes continue to ring even with damper engaged. Solution: Check to see that pedal adjustments are set correctly. If so, consider purchasing silicone-filled damper pads designed to correct this problem. The pads are available on the internet and also through percussion specialty stores.

Check vibraphone pedal mechanism for proper adjustment and tighten all wing nuts. Repeat the procedure for the tubular chimes.

Triangle

Triangles need little care, save for wiping them clean with a damp cloth. Triangle clips need constant repair. Check existing clips for worn or missing loops. Replace loops as needed using new fishing line. It is always a good idea to increase the amount of triangle clips and beaters available during your annual 'end of year' inventory. For new beaters, buy 3/16th inch drill rod lengths from local hardware store and cut into 8 inch segments. Burnish ends to remove any roughness. Build new clips from "No. 1" hardware store clamps.

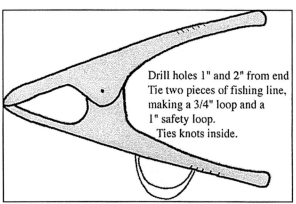

Drill holes 1" and 2" from end
Tie two pieces of fishing line, making a 3/4" loop and a 1" safety loop.
Ties knots inside.

Tambourine

Check tambourine heads and jingles. If pins holding jingles are working out, tap them back in with a small hammer and place a drop of household glue over end of pins. If the head is broken, replace as follows: Purchase tambourine replacement kit which consists of a calfskin replacement head and oversized rubber band. Soak head in tepid water for at least 20 minutes. While head is soaking, remove remaining pieces of broken head and any tacks or staples. Lightly sand bearing edge of shell until all the old, dry glue is removed. Apply a thick, even coat of carpenter's (or Elmer's) glue to sanded edge. Remove soaking head from water and pat dry. Center head over the tambourine so that any excess head extends at least one inch past the shell. Stretch the rubber band over head and rim and attach head to rim. Pull out the slack to make the head somewhat taut and adjust the rubber band so that it is even and near the top edge of the shell. Allow the tambourine head to slowly dry. When almost dry, use a single-edged razor blade, or razor blade knife, to trim excess head. Do this with great care! Allow head to fully dry and add tacks, if so desired.

Castanets

Check tie material on castanets, both hand and machine. Replace with round elastic cord (available from fabric stores). Adjust tension so chips respond correctly.

Temple blocks, Wood blocks and Slit Drums

Both temple blocks and wood blocks develop cracks. They can sometimes be repaired by filling the cracks with carpenter's cement. Force as much cement as possible into the crack. Wipe off excess. Use hardware store C-clamps, or wood working clamps, to hold crack shut until cement is good and dry. For broken slit drum tongues, it is best to remove and replace entire top of drum (if box-style drum).

Crotales, Gongs and Tam Tams

Check crotales, gongs and tam tams for cracks. Crotale cracks are difficult to see, but easy to hear (instrument loses its resonance). Replace all items that are cracked, since it is almost impossible to repair these bronze instruments. Check suspension cords on gongs and tam tams. Replace worn cord and tie knots securely. Check crotale rack for missing wing nuts and worn, or missing, insulators. Replace as needed.

Stands and Other Hardware/Equipment

Annually check all stands and other hardware to see if they are functional. Straighten all bent support rods and braces. Tighten loose rivets with hammer and punch. Replace any missing wing nuts and insulators. Clean dirt and grime from hi-hat and bass drum pedals. Oil where appropriate.

WORKS CITED

Beck, John H. 1995. *Encyclopedia of Percussion.* New York: Garland Publishing, Inc.

Blades, James. 1970. *Percussion Instruments and their History.* New York: Frederick A. Praeger, Publishers.

Blades, James and Jeremy Montagu. 1977. *Early Percussion Instruments From the Middle Ages to the Baroque.* London: Oxford University Press.

Buchet-Chastel, Corréa. 1956. "Musique nouvelle" trans. Derek Coltman. Quoted in Fernand Ouellette's *Edgard Varèse.* New York: The Orion Press, 1968.

Kastner, Kathleen Sherry. "The Emergence and Evolution of a Generalized Marimba Technique." (D. M. A. Thesis, University of Illinois at Urbana-Champaign, 1989)

Marcuse, Sibyl. 1964. *Musical Instruments A Comprehensive Dictionary.* Garden City, New York: Doubleday & Company, Inc.

The New Grove Dictionary of Music and Musicians. 2d ed, London: Macmillan, 2001

Payson, Albert and Jack McKenzie. 1976. *Percussion in the School Music Program.* Park Ridge, Illinois: Payson Percussion Products.

Peinkofer, Karl and Fritz Tannigel. 1976. *Handbook of Percussion Instruments.* trans. Kurt and Else Stone. London: Schott.

Pollack, Peter F. "The Forming of a Literature for the Solo Drum Set." (D.M.A. Thesis, University of Illinois at Urbana-Champaign. 2000)

Randel, Don Michael, ed., 1986. *The New Harvard Dictionary of Music.* Cambridge/London: The Belknap Press of Harvard University Press.

Rossing, Thomas D. 1982. Chimes and Bells. *Percussive Notes Research Edition.* (19, no. 3): 42-49.

Stone, Kurt. 1980. *Music Notation in the Twentieth Century.* New York: W. W. Norton.

Percussion Resources

Professional Societies

Percussive Arts Society
32 E. Washington, Suite 1400
Indianapolis, IN   46204

Annual membership in the Society includes subscriptions to *Percussive Notes* and *Percussion Newsletter*. The 2007 dues for professionals were $90.- for libraries $100.- for students $60. Student electronic memberships (ePAS) are available for $28. The Society is a non-profit organization and has been in existence since 1961. Its web-site (**www.pas.org**) provides members access to articles from past *Percussive Notes* and serves as an important source of information.

Percussion Periodicals

Percussive Notes
Percussive Notes is part of the Percussive Arts Society's membership benefits and is published bimonthly in magazine format. Columns include focus on education and other information of interest and use to music educators at every grade level. Reviews of new music and product advertisement are part of each issue.

Percussion Newsletter
The Percussion Newsletter is part of the Percussive Arts Society's membership benefits and is published during the months that the magazine *Percussive Notes* does not appear. *Percussion Newsletter* includes Society information, late-breaking news, product information and classified advertisements.

Reference books

Percussion Anthology
The Instrumentalist
1418 Lake Street
Evanston, IL 60204

The anthology contains percussion articles extracted from back issues of the magazine, *The Instrumentalist*, written between 1946 and 1977. Though many of the articles include dated information, the anthology includes valuable basic information for school orchestra and band directors.

Percussion Education: *A Source Book of Concepts and Information*
Percussive Arts Society
32 E. Washington, Suite 1400
Indianapolis, IN   46204

Practical materials designed to assist both music educator and percussion instructor. Contains recommended inventory lists for bands and orchestras of various levels.

Retail catalog sales

Steve Weiss Music
2324 Wyandotte
Willow Grove, PA 19090
(215) 329-1637

Catalog includes music, instruments, drum heads and other accessories. The music listing is extensive and includes the level of difficulty. A good source for price comparison with local and state music suppliers. Call for latest catalog since prices change annually.

Pedagogical Material

Snare Drum: (Elementary) Al Payson. *Beginning Snare Drum Method* with two play-along CDs; S. Feldstein & D. Black. *Alfred's Drum Method, Book 1.* Van Nuys, 1987; (Intermediate) *NARD Drum Solos.* Cleveland: Ludwig Music; (High School) Morris Goldenberg. *Modern School for Snare Drum.* New York: Chappell Music

Mallet-Keyboard: (Elementary) *Elementary Marimba and Xylophone Method* by Al Payson (Payson Percussion Products); *Tunes for Mallet Percussion* by Sandy Feldstein (Adler Pub.); (Intermediate) Linda Pimental & James L. Moore. *The Solo Marimbist, Vol. I.* Columbus: Permus Publications - (High School) Morris Goldenberg. *Modern School for Marimba and Xylophone.* New York: Hall Leonard Pub.

Timpani: (Elementary) Thomas McMillan *Basic Tympani Technique*; (Intermediate) Garwood Whaley Musical *Studies for the Intermediate Timpanist.* Joel Rothman Pub. - (High School) Saul Goodman. Modern School for Tympani. New York: (Technique only) Mervin Britton. *Timpani Tuning.* Belwin/Mills

Bass Drum: Al Payson. (High School) *Techniques of Playing Bass Drum, Cymbals and Accessories.* Northbrook: Payson Percussion Products

Cymbals: Sam Denov. (High School) *The Art of Playing Cymbals.* Belwin/Mills Pub.

Tambourine, etc.: (High School) Paul Price. *Techniques and Exercises for Playing Triangle, Tambourine and Castanets.* Music for Percussion (1955)

Drum Set: (Elementary) Gérard Berlioz. *La Petite Batterie D'Olivier.* Edition Combre - (Intermediate) Ted Reed. *Progressive Steps for the Modern Drummer.* Ted Reed Pub. - (High School) Jim Chapin *Advanced Techniques for the Modern Drummer Vol. I*

Recommended Ensembles

Elementary:
Boom-Whap - (sextet) xylophone, tambourine, snare drum, tom-tom, bass drum, timpani (2); Cirone: CPP/Belwin

Drums Galore - (sextet) bongos, snare drum, tom-toms (2), tenor drum, bass drum, timpani (2); Cirone: CPP/Belwin

Fugue - (sextet) snare drums (2), tambourine, bass drum timpani (2), tenor drum; Cirone: CPP/Belwin

Gliding Along - (sextet) orchestra bells, xylophone, snare drum, susp. cymbal, bass drum, timpani (2); Cirone: CPP/Belwin

March Right In - (sextet) snare drums (2), tenor drum, cymbals à2, bass drum, timpani (2); Cirone: CPP/Belwin

Nervous Notes - (sextet) tambourine, wood block, snare drum, claves, bass drum, tenor drum; Cirone: CPP/Belwin

Percussion Ensembles - (collection, 4 or more players) timpani, snare drum, bass drum, any mallet instruments; Feldstein: Belwin

Holiday Suite for Percussion - (trio) triangle, susp. cym, toms (3), tambourine, bass drum; Spears: Barnhouse

Intermediate:
A Little Song - (sextet) orch.bells, xylo., triangle, susp. cymbal, snare drum, bass drum, timpani (2); Cirone: CPP/Belwin

Allegro Fantastica - (quartet) snare drum, toms (2), triangle, woodblock, sus. cym, timpani (2); Spears: Kendor

Scamper - (quintet) tom-toms (4), snare drum, bass drum susp. cym, woodblock, timpani (2); Spears: Barnhouse

Woven Tales - (octet) bells, xylo., marimba, chimes, vibes (or piano), timpani (4), susp. cym., toms (4), triangle, susp. cym., snare drum; Spears: Barnhouse

A Time for Jazz - (octet) bells, xylo., marimba, vibes, chimes, timpani (4), toms(2), bongos, drum set; Spears: Southern

Mosaics - (sextet) snare drum, toms (4), tambourine, woodblock, susp. cym., bass drum, triangle, timpani (2); Spears: Barnhouse

Polyphonies - (quartet) snare drum, toms (4), timpani (4), bass drum; Spears: Southern

Advanced:
Dynamo! - (quintet) xylo., woodblock, triangle, marimba, toms (4), vibraphone(or piano) susp. cym., timpani (2), snare drum; Spears: Barnhouse

Romantique - (octet) bells, xylo, marimba, vibes(or piano), chimes, timpani (4), triangle, maracas, windchimes, snare drum, toms (4), susp. cym.; Spears: Southern

Windstone Suite - (octet) bells, xylo, marimba, chimes, vibes(or piano), timpani (3), triangle, snare drum, windchimes, susp. cym., toms (4), temple blks.; Spears: Barnhouse

Ceremonium - (octet) bells, xylo, marimba, chimes, timpani (2), triangle, snare drum, susp. cym., temple blocks, tom-toms (3), tambourine; Spears: Barnhouse

Bayport Sketch - (nonet) xylo., bells, marimba I, marimba II (opt.), chimes, vibes (or piano), timpani (2), susp. cym., toms (2), snare drum; Spears: Barnhouse

PERCUSSIVE ARTS SOCIETY INTERNATIONAL DRUM RUDIMENTS

ALL RUDIMENTS SHOULD BE PRACTICED: OPEN (SLOW) TO CLOSE (FAST) TO OPEN (SLOW) AND/OR AT AN EVEN MODERATE MARCH TEMPO.

I. ROLL RUDIMENTS

A. SINGLE STROKE ROLL RUDIMENTS

1. SINGLE STROKE ROLL *

2. SINGLE STROKE FOUR

3. SINGLE STROKE SEVEN

B. MULTIPLE BOUNCE ROLL RUDIMENTS

4. MULTIPLE BOUNCE ROLL

5. TRIPLE STROKE ROLL

C. DOUBLE STROKE OPEN ROLL RUDIMENTS

6. DOUBLE STROKE OPEN ROLL *

7. FIVE STROKE ROLL *

8. SIX STROKE ROLL

9. SEVEN STROKE ROLL *

10. NINE STROKE ROLL *

11. TEN STROKE ROLL *
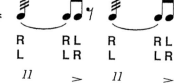

12. ELEVEN STROKE ROLL *

13. THIRTEEN STROKE ROLL *

14. FIFTEEN STROKE ROLL *

15. SEVENTEEN STROKE ROLL

II. DIDDLE RUDIMENTS

16. SINGLE PARADIDDLE *

17. DOUBLE PARADIDDLE *

18. TRIPLE PARADIDDLE

19. SINGLE PARADIDDLE-DIDDLE
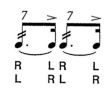

PERCUSSIVE ARTS SOCIETY

III. FLAM RUDIMENTS

20. FLAM *
L R R L

21. FLAM ACCENT *
L R L R R L R L

22. FLAM TAP *
L R R R L L L R R R L L

23. FLAMACUE *
L R L R L L R
R L R L R R L

24. FLAM PARADIDDLE *
L R L R R R L R L L

25. SINGLE FLAMMED MILL
L R R L R R L L R L

26. FLAM PARADIDDLE-DIDDLE *
L R L R R L L R L R L L R R

27. PATAFLAFLA
L R L R R L L R L R R L

28. SWISS ARMY TRIPLET
L R R L L R R L
R L L R R L L R

29. INVERTED FLAM TAP
L R L R L R L R L R L R

30. FLAM DRAG
L R L L R R L R R L

IV. DRAG RUDIMENTS

31. DRAG *
L L R R R L

32. SINGLE DRAG TAP *

L L R L R R L R

33. DOUBLE DRAG TAP *

L L R L L R L R R L R R L R

34. LESSON 25 *

L L R L R L L R L R
R R L R L R R L R L

35. SINGLE DRAGADIDDLE
R R L R R R L L R L L

36. DRAG PARADIDDLE #1 *

R L L R L R R L R R L R L L

37. DRAG PARADIDDLE #2 *
R L L R L L R L R R L R R L R R L R L L

38. SINGLE RATAMACUE *
3   3
L L R L R L R R L R L R

39. DOUBLE RATAMACUE *

3   3
L L R L L R L R L R R L R R L R L R

40. TRIPLE RATAMACUE *

3   3
L L R L L R L L R L R L R R L R R L R R L R L R

FOR MORE INFORMATION ON BECOMING A MEMBER OF THE PERCUSSIVE ARTS SOCIETY CONTACT PAS AT:
110 W. WASHINGTON STREET, SUITE A, INDIANAPOLIS, IN 46204 • E-MAIL: PERCARTS@PAS.ORG WEB SITE: WWW.PAS.ORG